Passio Christi

Passio Christi

MEDITATIONS FOR LENT

by Mother St. Paul

Laudamus press

Cover image: *Christ Carrying the Cross* by Titian, c. 1565,
housed at the Museo Nacional del Prado in Madrid, Spain.

Cover design by Mary Jo Loboda

Interior illustrations reprinted from the Campion Missal and Hymnal.
Used by permission. www.ccwatershed.org

Laudamus Press
P.O. Box 251
Hamlin, PA 18427
www.laudamus-te.com

Preface

MEDITATION! a word that frightens many. Nor is the alarm diminished by the explanation that meditation is an exercise of the three powers, memory, understanding, and will. Such set exercise is termed unnatural and wooden. Yet it is quite a natural proceeding. Thus the *memory* asks: What do I *know* about this subject, *e.g.* the Transfiguration? Let me recall all I know. Then the *understanding* comes in: What does it all mean? Then the *will* exercises itself in aspirations, affections, and acts of the several virtues. Particularly may be recommended acts of faith, adoration, and thanksgiving, a singularly profitable exercise in these days of diffidence and doubt. The will, likewise, forms practical resolutions, not always, and never too many. The whole ends with petition, asking for what I want, or rather, the whole should be saturated throughout with petitions. Such is the method of St Ignatius. It is exemplified in St Augustine's *Confessions*. And on this method these Meditations are, drawn up.

I am afraid some of us will be tempted to say they insist too painfully on the doctrine of the Cross. What else can you expect from *Passio Christi*? But we timid readers may take heart After all, suffering may, nay must, come upon us, and we never can tell in what measure. If we have mastered the doctrine of the Cross, we shall be forearmed. We shall not fret and repine, because we shall have learnt that there is good in suffering. Then what of the daily worries of life, too trifling to be called sufferings, yet often too much for our patience and our fortitude? Would it not be better for us personally, better for all those with whom we come in contact, if we bore up more bravely, and did our duty with less complaining? That again we learn of *Passio Christi*.

A Meditation Book is a good servant, but a bad master. We should not be slaves of our book. In using the book overnight to prepare our morning meditation, we should read in the corresponding part of the New Testament, and arrange our own points. This little book also will make good spiritual reading for Lent. It is the work of one who witnesses much of the good done by meditating. The House of Retreats, Birmingham, of which the authoress is in charge, is famous throughout the Midlands for the excellent results obtained by Week-end Retreats.

JOSEPH RICKABY, S.J.

Rosary Sunday, 1917.

Contents

Passio Christi

Before Meditation

1. *Recall vividly the Presence of God.* I am always in it, but I want, now, to shut out everything else, and to be, as it were, *alone* in it.
2. A prayer to the *Holy Ghost.*
3. *"The Preparatory Prayer is* to ask Our Lord for grace, that all my intentions, actions, and operations may be ordained purely to the service and praise of His Divine Majesty" (St Ignatius).

The Meditation

The Subject, Preludes, and Points have been fixed the night before; so, having recalled them, I apply my memory, my understanding, and my will to the First Point, interspersing many Colloquies, and passing on to the other Points, if my time (a fixed one) allows.

I am not obliged to remain kneeling for my Meditation. St Ignatius advises the posture in which the body will best aid the soul to meditate, whether kneeling, sitting, standing, or lying; but having chosen my position, he advises me not "to try any other," so long as I am doing well, for fear that restlessness should hinder the work on hand.

After Meditation

Kneeling down, I make my final Colloquy, my Resolution, and Spiritual Bouquet; and then I finish with these prayers, or any others that I prefer:—

Our Father, etc.　　　Hail Mary, etc.

Soul of Christ, sanctify me;
Body of Christ, save me;
Blood of Christ, inebriate me;
Water from the side of Christ, wash me;
Passion of Christ, strengthen me;
O good JESUS, hear me;
Within Thy wounds, hide me;
Suffer me not to be separated from Thee;
From the malignant enemy, defend me;
In the hour of my death, call me,
And bid me come unto Thee,
That with Thy saints I may praise Thee
For all eternity. Amen.

O Beloved Word of GOD, teach me to be generous; teach me to serve Thee as Thou deservest; to give, and not to count the cost; to fight, and not to heed the wounds; to toil, and not to seek for rest; to labour, and not to ask for any reward, save that of knowing that I do Thy Will.

Take, O Lord, and receive my liberty, my memory, my understanding, and my will—all that I have and possess. Thou has given me all these things; to Thee, O Lord, I restore them; all are Thine, dispose of them according to Thy Will. Give me only Thy love and Thy grace, for these are enough for me.

Examen on the Meditation

(For use some time during the day)

1. What was the subject?
2. Was it prepared last night?
3. What was the grace asked?
4. What was the principal thought?
5. With whom was the Colloquy?
6. What was the Resolution?
7. Was the Meditation successful? If not, why not?

From the *Campion Missal and Hymnal*

"Behold, We Go up to Jerusalem"

Quinquagesima Sunday.

"Behold, we go up to Jerusalem, and all things shall be accomplished which were written by the prophets concerning the Son of Man." (From the "Gospel" for today, St Luke xviii. 31.)

1ˢᵗ Prelude.   Jesus saying these words to the Twelve.
2ⁿᵈ Prelude.   Grace not only to "understand," but also to "go up" with Him.

Point I.
"Behold, we go up"

His Hour is approaching. His purpose is fixed. Jerusalem and Calvary are before Him. It is time to talk about it all, seriously, to His disciples. He had tried to break it to them, at least three times before, (chaps, ix. 22, xii. 50, xvii. 25), but they do not seem to have taken it in. Now He must speak more plainly. He would like them to know that the end is very near, (1) because He wants their sympathy, and (2) because they, too, will have to suffer, and He wants to prepare them. And so He says "Behold, *we* go up." We are going to face it together—you *with Me.*

I am one of His disciples, that is, one of those who are pledged to take up the cross and follow Him. Am I ready to be included in that *"we"*?—ready to go and suffer with Him this Lent? He is taking me apart now during my Meditation, as He took His disciples, (Matt. xx. 17), and saying to me: "Behold, we go up—are *you* coming?"

5

POINT II.

"ALL THINGS SHALL BE ACCOMPLISHED"

Having secured their attention by showing them that they are to have a part in it all, He tells His disciples what is going to happen, "The Son of Man shall be delivered to the Gentiles, and shall be mocked, and scourged and spit upon; and after they have scourged Him, they will put Him to death." (verses 32, 33.) It is the first time He has mentioned that He is to suffer at the hands of the *Gentiles*—a terrible thought for a Jew. It is the first time that He has gone into detail about His sufferings. He spreads out the terrible list before His disciples, mentioning, perhaps, the things He dreads most; and thus He appeals to them.

Thus too He appeals to me today, when the Hour of Lent is so near. He spreads His sufferings once more before me, hoping to make more impression this time. He appeals mutely for my sympathy, consolation, reparation—to be expressed in the identification of myself with Him—even unto death—the death of the old man. He has appealed before—more than *three* times. Will He appeal in vain this Lent?

POINT III.

"THEY UNDERSTOOD NONE OF THESE THINGS"

Why? for He spoke so plainly. They were too material, too much absorbed in their own ideas of what He was going to do and to be. The idea of a suffering Messias did not appeal to them; they did not like the thought of suffering; they did not understand; they did not *want* to understand.

I cannot pretend that I do not understand. Why then do I shrink even now, when I am making this Meditation, at the thought of mortification, and penance, and Lent? Why do I half wish that He had not taken me apart and said to me:

Come up with Me this Lent? I understand perfectly what He means. I even know exactly what thing it is that He wants me to "go up" courageously to meet, for He has entered into details with me too. Can it be that it is the *will* that is lacking, that I, too, do not *want* to understand? do not *want* to "go up," and act against my nature? If so, I know what to do. No one ever shrank more than did my Master from the cup of suffering that lay before Him, and yet it is He Who says: "Behold, we go up." There was no shrinking in His *will*. I will try to copy Him. My will shall get the better of my poor, shrinking nature. I will say as He did: "Not my will, but Thine be done." O my JESUS, suffering and shrinking for me, yet bold and courageous for me too, I thank Thee for taking me apart and giving me this invitation to "go up" with Thee. I accept it now with my *will*. Trustfully, humbly, joyfully, I put my hand into Thine ready to "go up" wheresoever Thou dost lead me.

Colloquy with JESUS apart.

Resolution. To understand, at any rate, some of these things.

Spiritual Bouquet. "Behold, we go up."

Charity (I)

Monday before Ash Wednesday.

"He that loveth not, 'knoweth not God; for God is charity." (1 John iv.8.)

1st *Prelude.*   Exposition during the "Forty Hours," and the Carnival.
2nd *Prelude.*   The grace of Reparation.

POINT I.
"CHARITY IS PATIENT."
(FROM THE "EPISTLE" FOR QUINQUAGESIMA.)

"God is charity." He Who is exposed now on the Altar is God, *and He is patient.* What is He patient about? There are only two days before Lent begins, and many of His children are spending these two days in utter forgetfulness of Him, in pleasure, and in *sin.* And He is still patiently waiting for the souls of those whom He has done His utmost to win. He created them on purpose to get enjoyment and glory out of them. He loved them to such an extent that He gave His life for them, and now they are outside, sinning against Him. His sheep are lost in the wilderness, and Charity is ever seeking them with infinite patience.

What can *I* do?—I who have come to watch before the Blessed Sacrament, on purpose to do what I can. I can keep very close to Him during these days of pain. I can make frequent acts of love, reparation, and contrition. *I* gave Him the same sort of pain once, and He was patient with me. Now I give Him a different sort, and He is patient with me still.

O patient JESUS, teach me, as I kneel here before Thee, to love Thee enough to be patient—patient with myself, patient with others, patient with all the souls whom, for Thy sake, I am trying to save.

POINT II.
"CHARITY IS KIND"

How kind is the Heart of JESUS! He is, longing and yearning for men to come to Him. He is not "extreme to mark what is done amiss," but pitiful, ready to forgive all, if only they will come. "Father, forgive them, for they know not what they do."

"I thirst." What for, Lord? For the love of those who crucified Me. What infinite kindness! because there was infinite love.

What can *I* do? I can pray for all for whom He thirsted. I can give Him my love and sympathy, and quench His thirst whenever He turns to me saying: "Give Me to drink." And, for His sake, I can try to be kind. Oh, how much room there is for kindness in the world! Am I as kind as I might be in manner and word, as well as in heart and intention? Charity is kind. When I really love, I shall be really kind.

POINT III.

"CHARITY SEEKETH NOT HER OWN"

Everything was His own. The place at His Father's Right Hand in Heaven, joy, glory, the worship of the Angels. And He left all. He did not consider His own interests, because He was Charity, and Charity seeketh not her own. And when He came to earth, it was His Father's glory and the interests of men that He sought—never His own. How is He being repaid these days?

And I, who profess to copy Him in His unselfish love, what am *I* doing? Am I occupied with my own rights, my own interests, my own concerns? or am I going, for once, to put all these on one side, and to seek the interests of sinners, by pleading for them before the Altar Throne? So shall I touch His Heart, so shall I show Him real sympathy. So shall I make His interests mine, and prove to Him that I too "must be about the things of my Father." Only love can make me thus unselfish. "Charity seeketh not her own."

Colloquy with JESUS exposed on the Altar.

Resolution. To love Him enough to be patient, kind, unselfish.

Spiritual Bouquet. Charity.

— ❧ —

Charity (2)

Tuesday before Ash Wednesday

"Having loved His own who were in the world. He loved them unto the end." (St John xiii. 1.)

1ˢᵗ Prelude.   Exposition of the Blessed Sacrament.
2ⁿᵈ Prelude.   The spirit of Reparation.

POINT I.
"CHARITY BEARETH ALL THINGS"

Every kind of neglect, indifference, carelessness, blasphemy, outrage—Our Lord suffers all because He loves. He bears all things (1) for His Father's sake—to glorify Him; (2) for His own sake—to satisfy His excess of love, which nothing but an excess of suffering *could* satisfy, (3) "for us men and for our salvation"—for sinners outside, and for me, His friend, who am watching with Him—to make up for my unwilling suffering, my petty mortifications, my measured penance.

What can *I* do? I can whisper to Him that I mean to try to "fill up" some of "those things that are wanting of the sufferings of Christ," (Col. i. 24), which He has left on purpose, that I might have the privilege and the joy of partaking in His sufferings. (1 Pet. iv. 13.) I can tell Him that I *will* try to be a little braver, a little more energetic. It is all a matter of love. If I love, I, too, can bear all things.

POINT II.
"CHARITY HOPETH ALL THINGS"

JESUS hopes for much from His children as He waits for them on His Altar Throne. Why is He exposed there? That we may come and see Him, and hear Him begging for a refuge in our hearts, where He may be sheltered from all the coldness, and indifference, and forgetfulness outside. Does He get what He is hoping for from me? "all things"? nothing kept back? It is His love for me which makes Him so hopeful. I cannot disappoint that love.

What do I know about this hope which comes from Charity in my dealings with others? Charity hopes for the best; hopes that there was a good motive, even for a bad action; puts the best construction on things; finds a good side, even when it is difficult. It is hope that keeps Jesus from breaking the bruised reed—He *hopes* that it can be mended—and from quenching the smoking flax—He *hopes* that the life may still be saved. This is the Charity that "hopeth all things," and it is the Charity that He has shown towards me, *and* it is the charity that He would have me show towards others. If I love God, and my neighbour *for* God, I shall be quick to find out the hopeful side in him.

Point III

"Charity never falleth away"

It is impossible—just because it is charity. "Having loved His own . . . He loved them unto the end." (St John xiii. 1.) *His* love can never fail, but what about mine? Can He count on it, as on a bank that will never fail, where He can come and draw whenever He likes, and be quite sure of getting whatever He wants? Can He count on my *fidelity* to make up for the want of it in others? on my *generosity,* when He wants something done that nobody likes doing? on my *selflessness,* when He wants to use me for the salvation of a soul? Can He count on my constant acts of love, contrition, and self-denial? on my doing *all* to please Him? He can if I love, for "charity never falleth away."

O my JESUS, Whose love for me I know will never fall away, help me to love Thee more, help me to give Thee the kind of love that Thou dost want, help me to love souls with a love that never falls away, that is, with a zeal that stops at nothing. So shall I be Thy consolation during this Lent.

Colloquy with JESUS in the Sacrament of His love.

Resolution,—as to some particular thing that I mean to do this Lent to prove my love.

Spiritual Bouquet. "He loved me, and delivered Himself for me." (Gal. ii. 20.)

"Remember, man, that thou art dust"

Ash Wednesday

"O GOD, who desirest not the death, but the repentance of sinners... in Thy mercy vouchsafe to bless these ashes, which we intend to receive upon our heads, in token of our humility, and to obtain pardon; that we who know that we are but ashes, and because of our wickedness must return to dust, nay deserve to obtain of Thy mercy, pardon of all our sins, and the rewards promised to penitents." (Second Prayer for "The Blessing of the Ashes.")

> *1ˢᵗ Prelude.* The ashes being sprinkled on my head.
> *2ⁿᵈ Prelude.* That the ashes may be to me "a wholesome remedy, health of body, and support of soul." (First Prayer for "The Blessing of the Ashes.")

Why does the Church make her children begin their Lent by coming to kneel humbly before their Creator while ashes are sprinkled on their heads? It is because she wants them to remember three important Christian duties: (1) Penitence; (2) Humility; and (3) Preparation for death.

Point I.

Remember! and Repent

God desires not the death, but the repentance of sinners. The object of Lent is, that men, by considering the sufferings of Christ for them, may be brought to repentance. Ashes, under the Old Dispensation, were a sign of grief. Mardochai "strewed ashes on his head" when he heard of the cruel edict of King Assuerus against the Jews. (Esther iv. 1.) Job's friends sprinkled dust upon their heads, by way of showing their sorrow and sympathy with him. (Job ii. 12.) But ashes were generally a sign of sorrow for *sin*. The people of Ninive, when they had their wickedness brought home to them by the prophet Jonas, "sat in ashes," from the king on his throne to the humblest of his subjects, (Jonas iii. 6.) Even holy Job said: "I reprehend myself, and do penance in dust and ashes." (Job xlii. 6.) And Our Blessed Lord, speaking to the wicked cities of Corozain and Bethsaida, said: "If in Tyre and Sidon had been wrought the miracles that have been wrought in you, they had long ago done penance in sackcloth and ashes." (St Matt. xi. 21.) And so the Church puts ashes on our heads, and says: *Remember!* remember that you, too, have cause for sorrow. Those ashes that are being sprinkled on your head were Palms of victory once. What has reduced Christ's triumph to ashes? What but your sins? You who shouted: Hosannah! last Palm Sunday, you who were so full of good resolutions at the end of last Lent, what have you been doing since? *Remember!* and having remembered, *repent.*

This is what God desires at the beginning of this new Lent. This is what He is waiting for. He is longing to forgive, and to restore men to His favour. He is "not extreme to mark what is done amiss." He is not waiting to punish. No, He is waiting to be gracious, to show mercy. And so His first word to us this Lent is: *Remember!* What use am I going to make of this first warning? On the answer to this question may depend the whole of my Lent —yea, the whole of my eternity. Am I going to listen to the pleading voice, saying: "Turn ye, turn ye from your evil ways, why will you die"? (Ezech. xxxiii. 11.) Am I going to fall humbly at His Feet, and "remembering, say, I confess my sin," (Gen. xli. 9), and so "obtain the rewards promised to penitents"; or am I going to reject once more the gentle reminder, and go up to receive my ashes as a matter of course, trying not to think too much about what it means?

Point II.

Remember! and be Humble

"I will speak to my Lord, whereas I am but dust and ashes." (Gen. xviii. 27.) Abraham, though he "was called the friend of God," understood his position. In the presence of his Creator he felt himself to be but dust and ashes. "Remember, man, that thou art dust." And the remembrance is to make me *humble*. I am to remember my absolute nothingness, and God's infinite goodness in creating me. There were many others that He might have made out of nothing, but He passed them all by, and, for some special reason of His own, created *me*. What was that special reason? Have I found out yet? And if so, how am I fulfilling His designs for me? Must I not admit, as I try to answer these questions, that often I have frustrated His plans for me? that, instead of being grateful to Him for His creation of me, I have, in my pride of heart, dared to turn round and rebel against my Creator, saying: "Why hast Thou made me thus?" (Rom. ix. 20.) Why hast Thou planned this, or done that? Why hast Thou given this, or withheld the other? "O man, who art thou that repliest against GOD? Remember that thou art dust," and "be humbled under the mighty Hand of GOD." (1 Pet. v. 6.)

Let me determine that this Lent shall see me growing in humility, that is, in the patient bearing of humiliations. The saints *loved* them! I cannot attain to this, but I can try to be thankful for, instead of rebelling against, the numerous little things which are allowed to happen to me, on purpose to give me an opportunity of crushing self. When self is flat on the ground, so that all can walk over it, and trample on it, then I shall be humble! And to help me in the difficult task set before me, the Church says: "Remember your starting point—only *dust!*"

To help me further, I may recall the words: *"He* remembereth that we are dust." (Ps. cii. 14.) *He* does not forget; and He finds in the fact a reason for pity and leniency. He does not expect too much of *dust!* He knows how frail it is, and He treats it with infinite gentleness. If *He* makes such allowances for my weakness, need I be surprised at it, and discouraged by it? need I lose patience with myself over my repeated faults, and broken resolutions, and numberless fresh beginnings? *He* remembers that I am dust; is not that enough? Let me acknowledge, in all humility, my weakness; acknowledge that of myself I can do nothing, and thank Him that His strength is "made perfect in weakness." (2 Cor. xii. 9.) Then, even as St Paul did, I may glory in my weakness, because it makes His strength the more apparent. To Him *must* be all the glory; it would be absurd to attribute glory to *dust!* "When I am weak"—that is, when I am humble enough to acknowledge my weakness—"then am I strong." (verse 10.)

Point III.
"Remember thy last end." (Ecclus. vii. 40.)

"Remember, man, ... that unto dust shalt thou return." Remember that there is a moment coming when soul and body must be separated—when the soul will go back to Him Who gave it, to render an account of things done *in the body,* and the body will "turn again to dust." (Job xxxiv. 15.) *Remember!* says the Church. "Remember thy last end," and prepare for it. The whole of life should be a preparation for death—body and soul working hard for their salvation. "There is a time to die." (Eccl. iii. 2.) Let me never forget it—never let a day pass without thinking of that time, fixed as certainly as the time of my birth. "Give glory to the Lord before it be dark, and before your feet stumble upon the dark mountains." (Jer. xiii. 16.) St Peter advises us to "converse in *fear* during the time of our sojourning here." (1 Pet. i. 17.) Why should I fear? Because to fear is to *watch.* If the good-man of the house had no fear of thieves, he would not watch. St Gregory says: "To fear death before it comes, is to conquer it when it comes." But at the same time, God's children need "fear no evil" when passing through the dark valley, for the *sting* of death is *sin*; and those who die in grace will die with a *Deo gratias* in their hearts, if not on their lips. "Thanks be to God Who has given us the victory through our Lord Jesus Christ." (1 Cor. xv. 57.) "Blessed are the dead who die in the Lord," *blessed* because, during life, they remembered their last end.

But what about the body? It shall turn again to dust; but that is not its "last end." I cannot leave it there. Let me try to grasp the role of that part of me which is called my body.

It is true that it is of far less importance than the soul; it is true that it is the servant, not the master; it is true that it is the "house of clay," (Job iv. 19), not the tenant; it is true that it is the "earthen vessel," not the "treasure"; (2 Cor. iv. 7); and it is true that I have got to keep it in its place, and make it help and not hinder the work of my salvation. But it is also true that the soul is not complete without the body; the body has a most important part to play, not only in this life, but through all eternity. This body of mine has received the pledge of immortality through being the recipient of the Body and Blood of Christ. "Through the Body," says St Chrysostom, "I am no longer dust and ashes." The body has a glorious future before it. It has been redeemed as well as the soul, and the soul's salvation is only complete in the resurrection of the body. Let me raise my eyes, then, from the dust; and think of the time when my body shall be wakened by my joyous soul, which, groaning within itself, has been waiting for the redemption of its body, (Rom. viii. 23), waiting for the time when it should be *changed* from dust into a "body of glory," waiting to be a perfect man. "It hath not yet appeared what we shall be, but we know that when He shall appear, *we shall be like Him.* And everyone that hath this hope in him, *sanctifieth* himself." (1 John iii. 2, 3.) This is what the Church wants me to do when she bids me *remember.*

> *Colloquy.* "Remember . . . that Thou hast made me as the clay, and Thou wilt bring me into dust again." (Job x.9.)
>
> *Resolution.* To remember my last end today.
>
> *Spiritual Bouquet.* "Memento homo quia pulvis es."

— ❦ —

Charity (3)

Thursday after Ash Wednesday

"Lord, what wilt Thou have me to do?" "follow after charity."
(Acts ix. 6; 1 Cor. xiv. 1.)

1st *Prelude.*   Before the Tabernacle.
2nd *Prelude.*   The grace to follow after charity.

POINT I.
"IF I HAVE NOT CHARITY, I AM NOTHING"

"Lord, what wilt Thou have me to do" this Lent? This is the cry of my heart. I know—for St Paul says so—that it is possible for my faith to be unbounded; for my knowledge and intelligence to be so exceptional that I may "know all mysteries"; for my eloquence to be so remarkable that men say: "It is the voice of a God, and not of a man"; (Acts xii. 22); for my goodness to the poor to be such that I make myself poor to give to them; for my spirit of mortification to be so intense that I would gladly "give my body to be burned"; for my Lenten rules and resolutions to be perfect—and yet for all these things to count as nothing, because they are not founded on love. "If I have not charity, I am nothing." What, then, O Lord, wilt Thou have me to do?

My child, since you have learnt that love is the principal thing—that it is greater even than faith and hope, that it will be admitted into Heaven while its two sisters are dismissed at the door—*follow after charity*, make it your principal aim this Lent, pursue it, search for it in all that you do. Make your rules for Lent, plan out your mortifications, your penances, your acts of self-denial—but remember that they will only be acceptable to Me in proportion to the amount of love that they contain. And remember, too, that the percentage of love is wont to be higher in the secret acts that nobody ever hears of, than in the things that our own little world, whose opinion is so valuable to us, knows all about.

POINT II.

CHARITY ENDURES

Charity is the "best gift," the "more excellent way," "the greatest of these" three sister gifts. It will never end; and everything that it touches becomes immortal, and will last, like itself, for ever. If I can say of any action: "I did it out of love to GOD," there is something about that action that will last through all eternity. It may have been very badly and awkwardly done, it may have appeared absolutely pointless in the eyes of the world, it may have been in itself a failure and an evident mistake, nevertheless the love in it will save it, and will make it of priceless value—the verdict of JESUS will be, "*you, did it to Me.*" Enough—that poor, little, badly-done action, which everyone laughed at, and even despised, and which was such a fruitful source of mortification and humiliation, will last when the Heavens and the Earth have passed away, and when time is no more! Charity *endures.* Oh, of what priceless value it is! With this thought I will face my Lent. It is love, and love only, that I will "follow after." Love shall be written across all I do. In my Examinations of Conscience, my first question shall be: How much love has there been today—in that action, in that duty, in that word, that criticism, that suffering, that disappointment, that temptation—how much has there been in the day's work that will last? how much that JESUS will gather up and label: "*Done for Me*"?

Our Lord told St Gertrude that provided there is *love,* He is satisfied with such little things—a little act of contrition, an ejaculatory prayer for the Holy Souls, even a step, a movement, a word. I will then draw up my rules for Lent more carefully than ever, but through all the spiritual exercises, the penances, the mortification, there shall be one thing that I am following after—*love*.

> *Colloquy* with Him "Who loved me and delivered Himself for me."
> *Resolution.* To follow after Charity this Lent.
> *Spiritual Bouquet.* "Follow after Charity."

— ❦ —

How to keep Lent

Friday after Ash Wednesday

"Graciously favour us, O Lord, we beseech Thee, in the fast we have undertaken, that what we observe outwardly, we may perform with sincere minds." (The "Collect" for the day.)

1st *Prelude.* The crowd listening to the Sermon on the mount. (See the "Gospel.")

2nd *Prelude.* To glorify God in. the keeping of my Lent.

POINT I.
THE WRONG WAY TO KEEP LENT

The Church gives us a note of warning today, in both the "Epistle" and the "Gospel." It is not enough simply to *perform,* the three great penitential works of Prayer, Fasting, and Almsgiving. JESUS says in the "Gospel" for today: Take heed, there is a wrong way, as well as a right way, of keeping Lent. And in the "Epistle," the people complain that GOD does not seem pleased with their fasting and humiliation: "Why have we fasted, and Thou hast not regarded? Why have we humbled our souls, and Thou hast not taken notice?" (Isaias lviii. 3.)

And GOD tells them why. Because, "in the day of your fast, *your own will is found.*" You are fasting, it is true, and humiliating yourselves; the body is doing its penance well; but what about the soul? You are going on still in your wickedness; you are doing your own will, not Mine; you are leaving out, altogether, the penitential work of Almsgiving, because that would cost you something. Go, fast from your sins, your pleasures, your own will, "then shalt thou call, and the Lord shall hear; thou shalt cry, and He shall say: Here I am; for I, the Lord thy GOD, am merciful." (verse 9.) He is waiting for something which means a denial of self and its demands to be offered to Him.

In the "Gospel," Our Lord speaks of another way of Prayer and Fasting and Almsgiving, which is quite wrong too—and that is, doing them *to be seen of men,* and therefore as a satisfaction to self. Such "have their reward" (Matt. vi. 2)—men's approbation, and self-love gratified; but GOD is saying: "Is *this* such a fast as I have chosen?" (The "Epistle"); to sound a trumpet before you give an alms; to stand in the corners of the streets to say your prayers; to have sad and disfigured faces, so that your fasting may be noticed? If this is your way of keeping Lent, know that it is the wrong way, and that you will not get the reward of your Father Who is in Heaven, for this is not the fast that *He* has chosen,

POINT II.

THE RIGHT WAY TO KEEP LENT

"Is this not rather the Fast that I have chosen? Loose the bands of wickedness, undo the bundles that oppress . . . deal thy bread to the hungry, and bring the needy and the harbourless into thy house."(The "Epistle.") "Let not thy left hand know what thy right hand doeth, that thy *alms* may be in secret; when thou shalt *pray,* enter into thy chamber and shut the door; when thou *fastest,* anoint thy head and wash thy face." (The "Gospel.")

Secrecy, privacy, closed doors, a cheerful countenance—these are what Our Lord recommends; and they are much more likely to lead to reality and purity of motive than the Pharisaical methods which Our Lord condemns. (St Matt. vi. 5.) Penance loves secrecy; and if these three great Lenten duties are to partake of the penitential spirit, which alone can make them acceptable, they must be done in secret.

If I, then, would keep my Lent in the right way, I shall see to it that each prayer, each act of self-denial, each deed of charity is for my "Father Who seeth in secret." Then may I expect the promise made in the "Epistle" to be fulfilled: The Lord shall give thee rest and fill thy soul with brightness."(verse 11.)

Point III.

"What do you do more?"

What do you do more? Our Lord asks me. The *publicans* love, the *heathens* are charitable, the *hypocrites* pray and fast and give alms, what do you *more?* He evidently expects more from me, and He does not leave me in doubt as to what He expects: "Be you, therefore, perfect, as also your Heavenly Father is perfect." My standard, then, is a high one. My Lenten rule, my prayer, my alms, my fasting—all are means to an end, and that end is *perfection,* that by it I may glorify God. To bring glory to God is to be my first aim throughout this Lent. "Be perfect," is to be my marching order, not for my own sake, not with any thought of self, but because the more perfect I am, the more I shall glorify God, and give Him the pleasure which He intended to get out of me when He created me.

Colloquy with Him Who said, "I do always the things which please Him." (St John viii. 29.)

Resolution. To try to do the same this Lent.

Spiritual Bouquet. "What do you do more? Be perfect."

The Fasting in the Desert

Saturday after Ash Wednesday

"Be attentive, O Lord, to our supplications: and grant that we may celebrate with devout homage this solemn fast which is a wholesome institution to heal both our souls and bodies." (The "Collect.")

1ˢᵗ Prelude. JESUS in the desert.
2ⁿᵈ Prelude. The grace of "devout homage"—that is, of imitation.

We shall be in the spirit of the Liturgy as expressed in the "Collect" for today if we forestall tomorrow's "Gospel" and make our meditation on Our Blessed Lord's fast in the desert.

POINT I.
WHEN DID HE FAST?

(1) *At the beginning of His public life,* as a preparation for His great work—to show us that we are not only to prepare by *prayer* for the work that we have to do and for the undertakings that cause us anxiety, but that *fasting,* too, should form an important part of our preparation. The principle is: I want GOD to do something for me, so I will do something for Him. I am very anxious for someone's conversion, I have prayed for it perhaps for years; have I tried fasting—that is, self-denial, mortification, penance, and offered them to GOD for that conversion? It *may* be that GOD is waiting for that.

JESUS fasted for *my* conversion; let me copy Him in His zeal and self-sacrifice.

(2) *Just after His Baptism* and the descent of the Holy Ghost. *"Immediately"* after His Baptism, St Mark tells us, "the Spirit drove Him out into the desert." This is how love acts—forces the trial upon us, but gives special grace first. This is why in times of consolation we should prepare for desolation. It is not usually after these times of fervour and spiritual consolation that we think of fasting; we are rather disposed to dispense ourselves from anything so disagreeable as penance just then. Our Lord fasted as an example to us, let us copy Him also in the time He chose for it.

(3) *After His exaltation before men.* A Voice had just said: "Thou art My Beloved Son, in Thee I am well pleased." There was no need for JESUS to fear praise and success, but He is fasting for our benefit, not for His own, and He would teach us to counteract the danger of praise by seeing to it that the "old man" gets his share of mortification.

(4) *Before temptation.* It was "when He had forty days and forty nights" that the tempter came to Him, and He knew that he was coming. Again, He would have us learn that the best preparation against temptation, which we know is ever at hand, though it is always unexpected, is to keep the body under, to live a life of mortification and penance. He told His disciples once that there are certain kinds of devils which are never cast out except by prayer and *fasting.* (St Matt. xvii. 20.)

POINT II.

WHY DID HE FAST?

Besides the reasons on which we have been meditating, He fasted (1) Because He wanted to be "tempted in all things like as we are." (Heb. iv. 15.) He told us to fast and how to fast, but that was not enough. He must *do* it too, and *show* us how. His method is to fast in the desert, in secret, in the very midst of temptations and difficulties.

(2) To show us that silence, and solitude, and mortification are the surest means of preserving the gifts of the Holy Ghost.

(3) To teach us that fasting is a means of expiating sin, He fasted in expiation for our sins; we can do the same, We can, by our voluntary penances, as well as by the suffering which God sends us, make reparation to Him for the past, and pay off some of the debt which is against us for those sins whose guilt has been forgiven, but whose punishment still remains, and also for those venial sins which perhaps we have never troubled very much about. We can never be quite sure how we stand with regard to this debt—how much we have paid, and how much is still owing; but there is a method of paying which is a very safe one, there is a coin which is so big that we need have no fear about its efficacy, it "covers a multitude of sins." It is the one Magdalen used: "Many sins are forgiven her, because she hath *loved* much." (St Luke vii. 47.) Let our fasting and our penance be prompted by a love which is so great that it *must* make reparation to a God Who has "forgiven all that debt because we asked," and the balance is sure to be on the right side.

(4) To encourage us in our forty days of penance—that we may not feel alone, but may know that we are doing all with Him. It is this same thought which runs through the "Gospel" for today. If Jesus is with us in the ship, the winds will cease. As soon as He sees our efforts and that we are "labouring in rowing," that is, really in earnest about our Lent, He will not leave us alone, but will come to us walking on the sea of all our difficulties and troubles, and as He steps into the ship which is starting on its forty days' voyage, He says: "Have a good heart, it is I, be not afraid"; I fasted that you

might know that I understand all about it; keep your Lent with Me, and you will have nothing to fear.

Colloquy with Him Who, for my sake, fasted forty days.

Resolution. To spend my Lent in silence and solitude with JESUS.

Spiritual Bouquet. "He was hungry."

— ❈ —

The Temptation in the Desert

First Sunday of Lent.

"He that dwelleth in the aid of the Most High shall abide under the protection of the GOD of Heaven." (The "Introit," Ps. xc. 1.)

1st *Prelude.*   JESUS, the tempter, and the angels.
2nd *Prelude.*   Grace to stand by, and learn.

POINT I.

THE TEMPTER

"That great dragon, that old serpent, who is called the devil and Satan, who seduceth the whole world." (Apoc. xii. 9.) "Your adversary who goeth about as a roaring lion seeking whom he may devour." (1 Pet. v. 8.) He it was who dared to approach the All-holy Son of GOD in His retreat. Some have thought that He came in human form, and the expressions used in the Gospel perhaps favour the opinion—the tempter *"coming"* (*accedens,* approaching), *"took Him up," "left Him."* He came in deadly earnest; he had waited long for this moment—ever since he had been cursed for introducing sin into Paradise. He knew that the Son of GOD was to come in human form; events thirty years ago had made him uneasy; and now his suspicions have been aroused again, by what has taken place at Jesus' baptism. *Can* this be the Son of God? He comes to settle the question, if he can. If he can only succeed in making Him *sin,* all will be well; he will be at his ease again. And so he approaches Him with the words: *"If thou be* the Son of God." But Jesus does not reveal Himself, and it was probably not until after His Resurrection that Satan knew for certain Who He was.

Let me think for a moment how far the love of my Jesus for me goes. He allows the *devil* to approach Him because He would have me learn how to resist temptation. Think what it must have cost Him, the All-holy, All-pure, to let Himself be in actual contact with the devil! What an insult, what a humiliation! And this to merit grace for me to overcome my temptations, and to teach me to receive humiliations meekly.

Point II.

The Temptations

(1) To *sensuality,* and *want of submission* to God's will. Turn these stones into bread, be a little indulgent to your body, take matters into your own hands and forestall God's plans a little, what does it matter? The answer is decisive: "It is written: Not in bread alone doth man live, but in every word that proceedeth from the mouth of God." Jesus shows by His answer His perfect confidence in His Father's arrangements, and that His will is more to Him than bread, but He does not make known to the devil His identity.

(2) To *presumption,* and *pride.* Jesus had professed His confidence in God, and it is on this profession that the devil founds his next temptation. "If Thou be the Son of God"—still he tries to find out—"cast Thyself down" from this pinnacle, God's angels will take care of you—it says so, *It is written.* The devil quotes, but he misquotes. The Psalm (xc. 11) says:

"He hath given His angels charge over Thee to keep Thee *in all Thy ways.*" The devil leaves out this last clause, because he knows that to throw Himself down from the pinnacle of the Temple would not be one of "His ways." If JESUS would work the miracle, it would certainly prove His Divinity; but if He is merely man, He would be yielding to the sin of presumption—so argues the devil. But he is foiled again, and is no nearer to finding out. It is written again: "Thou shall not tempt the Lord Thy GOD"—that is, Thou shalt not *test* Him to see whether His power and will are strong enough—in other words, Thou shalt not *doubt* Him.

(3) To *avarice,* and *ambition,* satisfied by *idolatry.* The devil showed Him all the kingdoms of the world and said: "All these will I give Thee, if Thou wilt adore me." Once more he hopes that if JESUS is the Son of GOD, He will assert His right to be adored rather than to adore. But JESUS meets him with the simple answer: "It is written: The Lord thy GOD shall thou adore, and Him only shalt thou serve." And the devil left Him—vanquished, puzzled, unsatisfied.

"Begone, Satan!" Thus does Our Blessed Lord deal with the Arch-fiend—and thus am I to deal with him. There must be no hesitation, no arguing, no considering; but a prompt, bold, decisive resistance. Whenever I thus imitate my Master, the result will be the same—the devil will *depart,* but his departure will only be *"for a time,"* as St Luke (iv. 13) is careful to add. We must never think that we have done with him, or that any particular temptation is finished with. He has gone away to watch, to consider, to devise fresh methods and stratagems, which may succeed where the last have failed. Let us be at least as alert and business-like as he is, and by prayer and fasting brace ourselves up for his attacks.

POINT III.

THE ANGELS

"Angels came and ministered to Him." What a change of atmosphere! What a relief! Who has not experienced it? The great calm, after a temptation resisted—the almost felt presence of GOD and of His ministering spirits. Just as when, unhappily, the temptation has been yielded to, the presence of the devil and his evil spirits has been felt. Let us, in time of temptation, remember that the ministering angels are hovering, near, waiting, at the first sign of victory, to cheer and console, refresh and congratulate us.

How glad the angels must have been to be sent on this mission of mercy to their King! And I can minister to Him, too, this Lent if I will, by imitating Him in overcoming the temptations I meet in the desert.

Colloquy with JESUS, Who for my sake was tempted.

Resolution. To avoid the occasions of sin.

Spiritual Bouquet. "Angels came and ministered to Him."

The Three Temptations

First Week. Monday.

"Thou shalt not be afraid of the terror of the night, of the arrow that flieth in the day, of the business that walketh in the dark, of invasion, or of the noonday devil." (The "Tract" for yesterday, Ps. xc. 5, 6.)

1st *Prelude.*   JESUS with the tempter.
2nd *Prelude.*   Grace to stand by, and listen, and learn.

In this Meditation we are going to look more closely at the temptations themselves, and see exactly what were the pitfalls which Our Blessed Lord merited the grace for us to avoid.

POINT I.
"COMMAND THAT THESE STONES BE MADE BREAD"

So says the voice of the tempter, and especially now at the beginning of Lent when I am making little devices to cheat the body of some of its bread. *Don't,* he says, it is not necessary. Why suffer? with a word—or even less—you know that you can alter things; if you do not look after your body, how can you expect to be able to do the work GOD has given you to do? Say the word and have the bread. This is the temptation which JESUS in His first encounter with the devil merited grace for me to resist—a temptation to sensuality in all its forms—that is, in all the ways in which the body can tempt—desires of the flesh, curiosity, sloth, vanity, love of ease and comfort, sins of the tongue—anything that gives the body the satisfaction for which it craves. Turn the stones into bread and give the body its rights.

Or again, the tempter comes with the old temptation: "Why hath GOD commanded you that you should not eat?" (Gen. iii. 1); it is unreasonable, take things into your own hands. He put you here in this place of trial and temptation and suffering, it is true, and gave you a plain command, but it is time now to change matters. He *means* to give you bread; take it, and do not wait for Him. Ah how subtle! What did my Master do. Waited patiently refusing to raise a finger to alter GOD's plans; showing me that I can only *live* by following GOD's will, though the devil says: "You shall not die" if you follow your own.

My lesson, then, is to be content where GOD has placed me, and never to lose confidence in Him, however dark things may look. *He* put me here; it is His affair, not mine. He *can* give me bread. He *can* alter my circumstances if He likes; till He does, I will wait; it is by GOD's word and will that the soul of man lives, not by its own caprice. I will trust Him though He slay me.

POINT II.

"CAST THYSELF DOWN, FOR . . . HE HATH GIVEN HIS ANGELS CHARGE OVER THEE"

Since your confidence in GOD is so unbounded, accept this position of danger that is offered to you, cast yourself boldly into it regardless of the consequences. He will take care of you; has He not promised to give His angels charge of you, lest you come to any harm? Or again, you were in that occasion of sin yesterday and did not fall, surely there is no harm in going into it again today. The harm is just this— yesterday you could not help yourself, that is, GOD allowed you to be in it, but today, if you go, you go by your own free will, and you go at, your peril; it is not one of GOD's "ways" for you, and He will charge no angel to keep you from dashing your foot against a stone.

In all these temptations to presumption—counting on GOD's help in dangerous occasions, which I might have avoided; expecting Him to work miracles for me; asking for things which are not in the order of His providence; trying to imitate the Saints in their fasts and austerities, and in the *extra*ordinary ways by which they were sometimes led; let me recognize the tempter, trying to *cast me down,* and let me answer with my Master: "It is written: Thou shall not tempt the Lord thy GOD."

POINT III.

"ALL THESE WILL I GIVE THEE IF . . . THOU WILT ADORE ME"

"All these"—whatever it is that you would like to have, I will get it for you if you will pay the price—*adore me.* Just acknowledge, by accepting my gifts, that I have a right over you. It is a subtle temptation to self-love—to give self what it wants at any cost, even that of taking what is lawfully His from GOD, and giving it to the devil. Every time that we thus oppose our will to GOD's, we really worship the devil; we lay our will upon his altar instead of upon GOD's. And what do we gain by it? The passing pleasure which self-gratification brings, and then the remorse that comes from knowing that we have "turned our back in the day of battle."

How does my Master deal with this temptation? "Begone, Satan!" for it is written: "The Lord thy GOD shalt thou adore, and Him only shall thou serve." "*Him only*"—never self. This rule is quite sufficient to carry me safely through all the temptations of the desert.

Colloquy with JESUS, Who overcame for me.

Resolution. To "prepare my soul for temptation." (Ecclus. ii. 1.)

Spiritual Bouquet. "Resist the devil, and he will fly from you." (St James iv. 7.)

— ❦ —

"Who is this?"

First Week. Tuesday.

"When, He was come into Jerusalem, the whole city was moved, saying: Who is this? And the people said: This is Jesus the Prophet, from Nazareth of Galilee." (The "Gospel.")

1*st Prelude.*   Jesus riding into Jerusalem.
2*nd Prelude.*   Grace to answer the question: Who is this?

POINT I.
THE CITY AND ITS QUESTION

The city had heard the cheers of the multitude, which had accompanied our Lord on His triumphal ride into Jerusalem. It had caught the Hosannahs and the words of the Messianic Psalm: "Blessed is He that cometh in the Name of the Lord." "And the whole city was moved"—it was curious, excited, anxious. *Who is this* that makes such a stir, and of Whom *we* know nothing? The question had been asked ever since His birth. Herod had asked it in that same city; the doctors in the temple; many, no doubt, at Nazareth; the people who saw His Baptism; Satan in the desert; those who saw His miracles; His own Apostles; those who saw Him suffer and die; those who saw Him after His Resurrection. And the world, ever since, has been asking the same question. JESUS of Nazareth perplexes it. His Church perplexes it. Who is this Who founded a Society, whose unity and power no amount of opposition has been able to touch? The city is moved, but it loses its chance, and allows the question to go by unanswered—and *He* would have been so glad to have answered it! so glad to have explained!

Point II.
The Answer of the Multitude

"This is Jesus, the Prophet, from Nazareth of Galilee." The multitude knows Him well enough. They know His name and where He comes from. He has taught in their streets, healed their sick, spent Himself for them during the last three years. They cannot plead ignorance, they know more about Him than the city knows; but what use will they make of their knowledge? "Crucify Him!" will be their cry in a few days' time. Ah, the multitude is easily swayed. Their answer is true as far as it goes, but what is it worth? What use do they make of their opportunity? The multitude, as well as the city, lose its chance.

Let me pray today, not only for those who do not know Him, because they will not take the trouble to find out Who He is; but also for those who do know Him, and who, in spite of their knowledge, are "crucifying again to themselves the Son of God, and making Him a mockery." (Heb.vi.6.)

Point III.
My answer

"Who is this that cometh from Edom, with dyed garments from Bosra, this beautiful One in His robe, walking in the greatness of His strength?" He gives the answer Himself: "I that speak justice, and am a defender *to save.*" (Isaias lxiii. 1.) It is my Jesus, my King, riding into Jerusalem, His own city, to die for me. And He wants me at the beginning of Lent to recall it all, and to answer the question once again for myself: *Who is this?* I know so much better than either the city or the multitude. Yet it is not an unknown thing for me, too, to lose my chances sometimes. When He comes and makes suggestions, I do not always respond to them, though I know quite well Who it is. He wants His little ones taught, His sick attended to, His poor helped, His prisoners visited, His sad ones cheered, His mourners consoled, His lost sheep sought. And He appeals to me, for He wants to say to me one day: "As long as you did it to one of these My least brethren, you did it to Me." But I am a little apt to answer mechanically: "This is JESUS, the Prophet," and then to let the next thing that self wants sway me in another direction. Let me determine during this Lent to answer with the Bride in the Canticles: "This is my Beloved, and He is *my Friend.*" (Cant. v. 16.) *I* know Him, and when He comes to me with His appeals for help, when He comes in my Communions, in my Confessions, in my Meditations, in my daily duties, my companions, my difficulties, my temptations, with my heart full of faith and love, I will put the question to *Him*: "Who is this?" just for the joy of hearing Him answer, *"It is I,* I that speak justice, and am a defender to save." I have come to save you through *this* means. Do not lose your chance.

Colloquy. "Who is this? It is I, be not afraid."

Resolution. To have the question: "*Who is this*?" continually present with me today.

Spiritual Bouquet. "Who is this? This is my Beloved, and He is my Friend."

Elias and the Jumper Tree

First Week. Ember Wednesday.

"He ate and drank, and walked in the strength of that food forty days and forty nights." (The "Epistle," 3 Kings xix. 8.)

1ˢᵗ *Prelude.*   Elias under the juniper tree.
2ⁿᵈ *Prelude.*   Grace to persevere.

POINT I.

THE PROPHET'S DEPRESSION

The story of Elias and his fast is one of the two lessons which form the "Epistle" for Ember Wednesday, The other tells us how Moses got strength to fast forty days and forty nights. Perhaps one reason why Holy Church, has brought before us these two great pillars of the Old Dispensation today is that, having before us these vivid pictures of what GOD *can* do for those whom He singles out to do His work in the world, we may pray with more faith and intensity for those who are about to be consecrated to Him by the Sacrament of Holy Order.

Elias "was afraid, and went whithersoever he had a mind;" (verse 3); this accounts for our finding him sitting under a juniper tree in the desert. Elias was passing through a time of depression and fear—it was the reaction following on a great victory. He had had a tremendous day, the day before. Single-handed, on Mount Carmel, he had met the worshippers of Baal, with their four hundred and fifty priests, besides four hundred prophets of the groves. By calling down fire from Heaven to consume his sacrifice, he had forced the fickle people to confess: "The Lord, *He* is God; The Lord, *He* is God." Then had followed the slaughter of all Baal's prophets; then at his prayer had come the rain which had been withheld for three years on account of the people's idolatry—and then he had run before King Achab's chariot right into the royal city. All knew him—he was a great man, for he had done great things for GOD and for His truth. But he had an enemy in Queen Jezabel, the chief of Baal's worshippers, and she had sworn a vengeful oath to take his life. This is the explanation of his running away, of his sitting under the juniper tree, and "requesting for his soul that he might die."

How often is this picture a true one of ourselves! By GOD's help we have been enabled to do some piece of work for Him—all has gone well, and all are speaking well of us; then some *little* thing goes wrong, and we at once slink away under the juniper tree, inclined to give all up! How childish! and yet how common! When shall we have learnt the lesson that desolation follows close on consolation, and *be prepared* for it? When shall we have learnt that God so often allows failure to follow success—*not* to discourage us and make us "request that we may die," but that we may know that *He* is the Master and that we are His dependents, taking from His hands whatever He is pleased to give—consolation or desolation, success or failure. "I am the Lord, I change not," and it is in order that we may learn this grand truth that He so often changes our circumstances and plans, and surroundings.

"It is enough!" says Elias, and worn out, he falls asleep.

Point II.

The Prophet's Strength

He is awakened by the touch of an angel, who bids him "Arise and eat"; and he sees prepared for him "a hearth-cake and a vessel of water." God is always gracious—even when we are petulant and unreasonable. He knows that His servant is tired and worn out in His service, and He sends one of His own messengers to refresh him. Elias does not seem to think it strange. "He ate and drank, and fell asleep again." A second time the angel comes: "Arise and eat, for thou hast yet a great way to go; and he ate and drank, and walked in the strength of that food forty days and forty nights, unto the mount of God—Horeb." (verses 7 and 8.)

It is often so. Just when we have decided that things are too much, and that it is better to give all up, God wakes us up and brings us to our senses. How? By giving us another difficulty to be met, another trial to be borne, another temptation to face. He gives the necessary grace and strength, it is true, but with it the stern reminder: "Thou hast yet a great way to go." *There* is the difficulty and it has got to be faced, and its very presence, as it is meant to do, braces our faith and our courage, and makes us quit the juniper tree.

Do I not see my lesson? It is no use, GOD says to me, giving up at the first difficulty; you began your Lent well, made great efforts to put yourself in the Spirit of Holy Church, faced your temptations nobly—and now this depression just because you have failed! Lent is not over, "you have yet a great way to go." Arise and eat the Heavenly Food that I have provided. Know that the Blessed Sacrament is sufficient for every need. "In the strength of that Food" you will be able to go not only through the forty days of Lent, but all through your wilderness journey till you come to the true mount of GOD—the city which is above—the Heavenly Jerusalem.

Colloquy with JESUS, Who is ever ready to provide Food
for the journey.

Resolution. To walk in the strength of that Food day by
day, never doubting its sufficiency for every need.

Spiritual Bouquet. "Arise and eat, for thou hast yet a
great way to go."

— ❧ —

Dogs, Children, and Crumbs

First Week. Thursday

"As I live, saith the Lord God . . . ALL souls are Mine." (The "Epistle.")

1ˢᵗ *Prelude.* The woman of Canaan and JESUS. (The "Gospel.")
2ⁿᵈ *Prelude.* Grace to treasure, and also to be generous with, the crumbs,

Point I.
Dogs—the Woman

She is a Gentile—probably an idolatress. She is in great distress, for she has a daughter who is "grievously troubled by a devil." She has heard of the power of Jesus over the devil—is that power, she wonders, to be exercised only for His own people? She is only a "dog" (a name given to the Gentiles by the Jews), an outsider, but there can be no harm in trying. So she goes right up to Jesus, states her case, and asks for mercy. "Have mercy on me, O Lord, Thou Son of David, for my daughter is grievously troubled by a devil." And she waits humbly at His Feet.

No one is *outside* the Heart of Jesus who in trouble turns to Him. The desire of His Heart is that all such should come, and when they do, they will get, as this woman did, far, far more than they ask. If He is thus waiting to be gracious to those who know Him not, what is His tenderness towards His *children*! And yet I keep my troubles to myself, pretending that they are too small for Him to notice, or that it is no use telling Him! Children can learn many lessons from dogs!

"O taste and see that the Lord is sweet." (The "Offertory.")

Point II.
Children—the Disciples

"Send her away, for she crieth after us." So say the children. Children often behave so to dogs, especially: when they are begging for some of their food. And the Master does not rebuke them. Things do not look very hopeful, but *she* hopes. Now the Master is speaking, and He is evidently siding with the children: I was sent for the sheep, not for dogs. She interrupts Him with an agonised cry: "*Lord, help me!*" Did she see in His Face a look that belied the harshness of His words? But

He continues in the same strain. I cannot take the children's bread and give it to dogs! How *could* He treat her thus, He *Who* is so infinitely tender and gentle? Because His Sacred Heart was yearning for her, and the joy which she was even now giving Him was only increased by keeping her waiting. Just as a mother takes pleasure in pretending that she is not going to give the longed-for gift to her little one, not because she enjoys the momentary pang of disappointment which she is causing, but because of the enhanced joy there will be on both sides when she produces the gift. He saw her love and her desire, and He wanted to increase them; He knew that He could count on her, and that opposition and difficulty would only give her fresh courage. He wanted to whet her appetite. He wanted to try her that she might have all the more merit; He wanted His goodness to be the more marked on account of His apparent severity; and last, but not least, He wanted to teach her how infinitely precious is the children's bread. And so He says: "It is not good to take the children's bread, and to cast it to the dogs."

When I am inclined to think that my troubles and difficulties are "*endless*," as I sometimes say, let me recall a few of the possible reasons that the Sacred Heart may have for allowing them, apparently, to be so.

But the Master's treatment does not excuse the disciples. They were thoughtless, selfish, unkind, narrow-minded, and show me how I am *not* to behave to the "other sheep." The bread is mine, and I have a right to a place at the Master's table; but let me see to it that I never waste it, nor grudge it to others.

Point III.
Crumbs—the Bread of Life

She has found a way out of the difficulty, as women mostly can. She does not ask for the children's bread, her humility does not aspire to anything so great—*crumbs* will do for her, crumbs that the children drop and waste. And so with wondrous faith and hope she makes her last appeal. It is quite true, Lord, it would not be good to take the bread from the children, but *under* the table there are *little* dogs, and they eat the *crumbs*—the crumbs that *fall* by mistake from *their* master's table. What humility there is in every word! and what boundless confidence! for now she considers that He is *her* Master too, though she is only His little dog, underneath the table, looking for crumbs.

Her humility and her need have prevented her from noticing any rebuff on the part of either Master or disciples; and she, the idolatress, is now *"adoring"* her Savior. It is enough, the Sacred Heart asks no more; It is ever touched by humility, and It can wait no longer. "O woman, great is thy faith; be it done to thee as thou wilt." And she leaves His presence not only with her request granted, but raised to the level of the children with a right to sit at the Master's table, to eat the Bread of Life, and to live for ever.

Let us pray very earnestly, and do penance too, during these days of prayer and fasting, for the conversion of sinners and for the return to the fold of the "other sheep."

Colloquy with Jesus, Who is longing to give the crumbs to the "other sheep."

Resolution. To thank Him once again for the crumbs He dropped for me.

Spiritual Bouquet. "The bread that I will give is My Flesh, for the life of the world." (The "Communion.")

— ❧ —

A Pond called Probatica

First Week. Ember Friday.

"An Angel of the Lord descended at certain times into the pond, and the water was moved." (The "Gospel.")

1ˢᵗ Prelude. The pond, and the sick folk lying round, waiting.
2ⁿᵈ Prelude. The grace to want to be made *whole*.

POINT I.
THE SICK, THE BLIND, THE LAME, AND THE WITHERED

This picture, which the Church brings before us today, may be taken as representing the numbers who are waiting for the blessings of Lent. They have a consciousness that they might be better than they are, and that Lent is the time for effort. At "certain times" the Angel comes and troubles the waters. Lent is surely one of those times. So there are: (1) *The sick,* the languid ones *(languentes),* the lukewarm, those who know quite well that they are slack, careless, slothful about their spiritual life, and yet never seem able to make the effort to begin again, (2) *The blind* —those who cannot see the truth, who are always in difficulty about what they should do, where they should go, which is the right course to pursue, whether GOD really means just what He says; they are determined, if possible, to get a clearer vision of things this Lent, and to bring matters once and for all to a climax. (3) *The lame,* always halting, always falling, always sinning—and yet always getting up again and going on, or they would not be at the pond; such have every reason for hope. (4) *The withered (aridi),* the dried up; these have evidently been brought to the pond by their friends, for they could never have got there alone. They are the souls in

42

mortal sin, the many outsiders who are borne in the hearts of their friends during Lent. Oh, what a time it is for intercession for sinners, and what a harvest-time for confessions! Let us try this Lent, by our prayers, by our penance, and by our personal efforts, to bring many to the "fountain opened for the washing of the sinner." (Zach. xiii. 1.) For "if the wicked do penance for all his sins which he hath committed, living he shall live and shall not die, and I will not remember all his iniquities that he hath done." (The "Epistle.")

Point II

Jesus at the Pond

He makes straight for one of the languid ones *(languidus)*. Is it because their case is the most difficult, and perhaps the most dependent on something outside themselves to help them? He knew the man had already been thirty-eight years in that state, and that he had every appearance of remaining so to the end of his days. And so He puts a question: "*Wilt* thou be made whole?" He knew that the man would never get up enough energy to address Him. "*Wilt* thou?" do you desire it? The question is almost startling; the man has been in this state for so long, that he has almost ceased to think of any other as possible; he has to collect his ideas, and recall what being "made whole" means. He is, however, ashamed, for his first thought is an excuse: I have no one to help me, another always gets there first. JESUS answers: "*Arise,* take up thy bed, and walk." There is the word of power, and there is the languid man's opportunity. You can continue as you are, if you like, but it you want to be made whole, you must use effort. Others get there before you because they make efforts, you are left behind because you do not.

It is all so true of the lukewarm soul, the soul that has allowed itself to get slack first about one thing and then about another, till absence of effort, want of generosity, cowardice about self-abnegation, and about using remedies against evil tendencies, carelessness about occasions of sin, now form its *habitual state.* It is a terribly dangerous state, because the lukewarm soul is so accustomed to it that it does not recognize its danger, "Thou *knowest not* that thou art wretched and miserable, and poor and blind and naked," (Apoc. iii. 17), and hence the difficulty of the work of healing. Almighty GOD Himself seems, if we may say it reverently, at a loss as to how to deal with such a soul. "I would thou wert cold or hot, but—thou art *lukewarm*"! (verses 15 and 16.) Is there no remedy then? Yes—*effort.* Be *zealous,* and *do penance,* (verse 19.) *Arise* from this state of lethargy and indifference; *take up thy bed,* be no longer tied down to your lower nature, carry it instead of letting it carry you; be the master not the slave, and *walk* in newness of life.

The languid man was no longer languid, he corresponded to the grace offered, he made his choice, put forth effort, "*and immediately he was made whole.*" What am *I* going to do? The choice is put before me once more; once more the grace and the power are offered; once more I have the chance of rising out of this state of tepidity that GOD so detests. "*Wilt* thou?" That is the whole point. And GOD adds so pleadingly, "I *counsel* thee to buy of Me gold, fire-tried, that thou mayest be made rich and clothed in white garments." (verse 18.)

POINT III.
A WORD OF WARNING

"Who is that Man Who said to thee: Take up thy bed, and walk"? ask the Jews. The man could not say, for he had not recognised Him in the crowd, but he recognised Him a little later in the Temple, whither he went for his first *walk*. JESUS sought him there, for He had something more to say to him: "*Sin no more, lest some worse thing happen to thee.*" You have made a great effort, gained a great victory over self, made a good choice, raised your standard, *but* do not suppose that a state which has been habitual for thirty-eight years will disappear in an instant and never more assert its claims. No, again and again you will be tempted to lie down on that bed, which today you have so bravely carried. This effort that you have made in GOD's grace must by His grace be *sustained*. Watch and pray, or a worse thing may come to you; the question, "Wilt thou be made whole?" may never again be put; the moment of grace may be over; this Lent may be your last.

Colloquy with Our Lord, Who is saying to me: "Wilt thou be made whole" of that particular thing which thou knowest to be displeasing to Me?

Resolution. To make the effort, and to sustain it.

Spiritual Bouquet. "Arise, take up thy bed, and walk."

The Transfiguration (I)

First Week. Ember Saturday.

"*Jesus taketh Peter and James and John ... and bringeth them up into a high mountain apart, and He was transfigured before them.*" (The "Gospel.")

> *1ˢᵗ Prelude.* JESUS and the three Apostles climbing the high mountain.
> *2ⁿᵈ Prelude.* Grace to learn the lessons.

Point I.
The Ascent

Jesus chooses the three Apostles whom He so often has with Him on special occasions—the next time will be in the Garden. He treats them as real friends, and invites them to share His joys as well as His sorrows. Probably the ascent was made in silence, for their hearts were very full. Only six days before, Jesus had told His disciples that He was going to Jerusalem to suffer and to die, Peter, in his zealous love, had expostulated with his Master, saying: "This shall not be to Thee"; but he had received a sharp rebuke in return. Then He had spoken to them of the necessity of the cross for each one of them if they would be true disciples, and, lastly, He had said something about the Son of Man coming one day in His glory with the Angels, and that *some* of them should see a little of that glory *before they died.* It was all very puzzling, they could not understand much about it, but they were glad to be with their Master; perhaps He would clear things up for them.

We too, as we *go up* with Our Lord this Lent, have our puzzles, our fears, and our hopes. There are many things we cannot understand, many crosses we should like to avoid, many promises of glory which are too much for our hearts to conceive; but one thing we *can* do—keep close to the Master, turning over in our minds the things that He has told us, and waiting in silence till He explains furthers

Point II.
The Transfiguration

Arrived at the top of the mountain, Jesus went to pray, St Luke tells us, and His three companions fell asleep. (How like it is to the Garden!) Then Moses and Elias "appeared in

46

majesty" and talked with Him about the things that were uppermost in His mind—"His decease which He should shortly accomplish at Jerusalem." No doubt it was a consolation to Him to talk with these great saints of the Old Dispensation, though in the case of one of them the bitterness of death had been removed, (Deut. xxxiv. 1-7), and the other had not tasted death at all. (4 Kings ii. 11.)

Wonderful things are going on, and the Apostles are asleep! Perhaps it was the voices that woke them. What a sight met their eyes when they did wake—their Master's Face shining as the sun, and His garments white and glistening like snow. The cross and death were the thoughts they had gone to sleep with, and now they are dazzled by the glory! They do not understand yet; they will understand more as the days go on. Their faith will have need of this vision to aid it. When they see that Holy Face covered with blood and dust and spittle, will they remember how it shone on the mount? Will they remember those proofs of His Divinity so graciously given, and will the remembrance help them to bear the awful days that are before them? This is what the vision of glory was meant for. And this is what my times of consolation, my little bits of glory, are meant for. *They* did not understand. Do I? "Forget not the things that thine eyes have seen, and let them not go out of thy heart all the days of thy life." (Deut. iv. 9.)

POINT III.

THE CONVERSATIONS

Let us contemplate these conversations carried on by to representatives of the two Dispensations—The *Old,* Moses and Elias, representatives of the *Law* and the *Prophets* the *New,* Peter, representative of the great array of *doctors* James, of the noble army of *martyrs,* John, of those who follow the Lamb whithersoever He goeth, for they are *virgins.*

(1) Moses and Elias spoke of His *decease—excessum ejus.* The word used means a *going out,* and is a common word for death—a going out of life. But it is also used to describe any deviation from the normal—hence our English word *excess*—something that goes out and beyond what is necessary or normal. It was not then simply of His death that they held converse, but of the excesses of that death—of all the accompaniments which were so abnormal, so unnecessary, except to satisfy the excess of His love. "Could anything have been done that I have not done?" With Him is not only redemption, but "*copious* redemption."

If I am taking JESUS as my model this Lent, I ought to know something about this word *excess*—for His excesses began in the stable at Bethlehem and did not end till *after* His death, when a soldier with a spear opened His Sacred Heart—an action wholly unnecessary, but permitted to satisfy His love of excess. What does *my* love know about excess? I fear, if I begin to look into things, that I shall find that "as little as necessary" is far more often my rule than "as much as possible."

(2) Peter feels that he must say something, though "they were so struck with fear," St Mark tells us, that "he knew not what he said." "Lord, it is good for us to be here; if Thou wilt, let us make three tabernacles, one for Thee, and one for Moses, and one for Elias." Let us stay here always and forget all about the cross and the suffering.

How much more keen he was—and we are too—on the glory than on the cross. It is so difficult to learn the lesson that the one is the outcome of the other—that the cross leads to the glory, nay, is the cause of it. There *is* a crown laid up for me, but it can only be won by taking up my cross daily and following.

Colloquy with JESUS on the mount of Transfiguration.

Resolution. Not to forget to pray today for the complete transfiguration of those favoured ones whom Jesus has chosen and taken apart on to the high mountain of Ordination to give them a sight of His glory, and to put them into the closest possible contact with His Divinity.

Spiritual Bouquet. "Forget not the words which thine eyes have seen."

— ❧ —

The Transfiguration (2)

Second Sunday of Lent.

"Behold a bright cloud overshaded them, and lo, a, voice out of the cloud saying: This is My Beloved Son, in Whom I am well pleased: hear ye Him." (The "Gospel.")

1ˢᵗ Prelude. JESUS touching the prostrate Apostles and saying: "Arise, and fear not."

2ⁿᵈ Prelude. Grace to understand the intimate connection that exists between the cross and the glory.

POINT I.
THE VOICE

"They were afraid," St Luke tells us, "as they entered into the bright cloud"; and then came the Voice from Heaven proclaiming, in the same words as at His Baptism, that this was indeed the Son of GOD, and adding the words: *"Hear ye Him";* He must be listened to, and obeyed. It was a stupendous moment for the three Apostles. We cannot wonder that "hearing it, the fell upon their faces, and were very much afraid." Fifteen hundred years before Moses had heard that dread Voice and had said: "*Exterritus sum et tremebundus,*" I do exceedingly fear and quake. (Heb. xii. 21.) Elias too had heard it in the days of his mortal life, and though it was only like the soughing of a gentle breeze—"*sibilus auræ tenuis*" (3 Kings xix. 12)—he covered his face with his mantle in fear as he heard the words: "What dost thou here, Elias?"

But the Voice spoke to the representatives of the *Gospel* for the same reason as it had spoken to the representatives of the *Law* and the *Prophets,* namely, to strengthen their faith and to teach them their duty. It assured the Apostles that their Master's mission was Divine, and that His words—even those about His sufferings and death and the cross must be listened to—"In Him"—in all He does and says—"I am well pleased."

It is not only the Apostles who were "slow of heart to believe." My backwardness and lukewarmness about taking up the cross and following Him this Lent shows that I, too, need the reminder that it is JESUS, GOD's Beloved Son, Who bids me do it, and sternly the Voice from Heaven says: "Hear ye Him."

POINT II.

THE TOUCH

"JESUS came and touched them, and said to them: Arise, and fear not." How like Him! Even in this moment; when He might well for a brief moment forget earth and all its troubles, and stay listening to that Voice, which to *Him* was so full of consolation, He thinks of His poor, terrified Apostles, who did not dare to raise their faces from the ground for fear of what they might see. He came and *touched* them, to let them see that it was He Himself, the same as ever. *Arise,* there is nothing to be afraid of. It was only My natural state which

I allowed to be seen for a little moment, to strengthen you for all that lies before you. It is all over now; the Heavenly Visitors are gone; the Voice has said what it had to say. And *"looking about"* (St Mark) as if to assure themselves that all was natural again, "they saw no man, but JESUS only."

It is JESUS Who comes to touch me, too, in my Communions, in my Meditations, in my Confessions and Absolutions. Happy is it for me when I can see *JESUS only* in them. In my dealings with others too—in the sick I am nursing, in the poor I am visiting, in the children I am teaching, in the ignorant I am instructing, in the disagreeable people that I meet, in the uncongenial ones that I may have to live with—in all these my faith ought to be strong enough to recognize the touch of JESUS. What a help it would be, if when I *look about* on all these I could see no *man,* but JESUS *only!* Yet it could be so, for it is not only into visions of *glory* that JESUS transfigures Himself, but also into visions of sickness and suffering and poverty—yea, even the sinner may be a vision of Him.

POINT III.

The Descent

"As they came down from the mountain Jesus charged them saying: Tell the vision to no man." It is only for you—for your consolation; keep it ever present with you while you are witnessing My sufferings and carrying your cross after Me. And remember that "the sufferings of this time are not worthy to be compared with the glory to come." (Rom. viii. 18.) I have shown you the vision to help you to understand what an intimate connection there is between suffering and glory, and to what the Way of the Cross leads. Then he begins to talk to them again about His Passion—"The Son of man must suffer many things." (Matt. xvii. 12, 21, 22.) He wants to keep their minds fixed on the cross, while still they do not forget the glory. St Luke tells us that He added: *"Lay you up in your heart these words"* (ch. ix. 44). Is it possible that; they *could* forget the Vision, the Voice, the touch and the words of Jesus? When the trial comes, they will sleep during His agony. Peter, who thought it so good to be on the mount, will deny with an oath that he knows Him, and all of them will forsake Him!

Let me take warning.

> *Colloquy* with Jesus, Who So often gives me times of refreshing on the Holy Mount.
>
> *Resolution.* To try to recognize the touch of Jesus today.
>
> *Spiritual Bouquet.* "They saw no man, but Jesus only."

— ❧ —

The Traitor's Bargain

Second Week. Monday.

"What will you give me? and I will deliver Him, unto you." (Matt, xxvi. 15.)

We are now going to leave the Liturgy, or rather not to follow it so closely, and for the rest of Lent confine our Meditations to some of the wonderful things that took place during Our Lord's last week on earth, on the Sunday of that week He rode into Jerusalem—a subject about which we shall meditate on Palm Sunday—the nights He probably spent at Bethany, or in the Garden of Gethsemani.

1st *Prelude.*   The Council, held by the Chief Priests and Ancients, to discuss how they could get rid of Jesus.

2nd *Prelude.*   The grace never again to deliver Him up.

Point I
The Council

They were very much troubled about Jesus. Several attempts had been made on His life; all had failed. He either "escaped out of their hands," (John x. 39), or else His enemies were overcome by His presence, and could only say in answer to their masters' disappointed question: "Why have you not brought Him?" "*Never did man speak like this man.*" (John vii. 46.) Since He had raised Lazarus from the dead, there had been an organized plot against Him—"from that day they *devised* how they might put Him to death," (John xi. 53), "and the Chief Priests and Pharisees had given a *commandment* that if any man knew where He was, he should tell, that they might apprehend Him." (verse 56.) Still they are baffled. Now they are holding a consultation about it; they think that their object can only be gained by *subtilty;* it is time that something was done—that triumphal ride into Jerusalem on Sunday has done their cause no good; it has evidently turned the people in His favour; perhaps there will be "a tumult amongst the people" if any steps are taken now, especially during the Feast, when Jerusalem is full of strangers; it might be better to defer matters till after the Feast.

The princes are consulting together against the Lord and against His Christ (Ps. ii. 2). What for? "To do, O God, what *Thy* Hand and *Thy* counsel *decreed* to be done." (Acts iv. 28.) God had fixed the hour—it was to be *during* the Feast, and while the Princes are holding their puny little Council, Jesus is preparing to deliver Himself up, because His hour is come, just as He escaped before, because His hour was not yet come.

Oh, what a consoling thought! No plans of man—not even of Princes and Rulers, however carefully devised, can change God's plans, nor alter His time. When the powers of darkness seem to be let loose, and to be shaking the very foundations of the earth, the child of God may look up and say: "The Lord reigneth "—it is my Father who is on the throne, nothing can happen without His permission—and as for His children, the very hairs of their heads are all numbered.

Point II.

JUDAS

"And Satan entered into Judas, who was surnamed Iscariot, one of the twelve." (St Luke xxii; 3.) This explains—for nothing else could—the shameful transaction that is now about to take place in the Council. Judas had been irritated in the house of Simon the leper by what he was pleased to call *a waste* of precious ointment; it might have been sold, he said, for the benefit of the poor; but St John explains that he said this, because he was *a thief,* and having charge of the common purse, helped himself out of it when he liked. He was evidently in want of money just now, and he saw his opportunity in the dilemma of the chief priests. Bursting into the Council-room he demanded: "What will you give me? and I will deliver Him unto you." It was a moment of triumph for Satan and his hosts—but the angels veiled their faces, the scene was too terrible for them to witness—one of His own chosen apostles—*a traitor!*

The agreement was soon made. It was exactly what the chief priests wanted—"they appointed him thirty pieces of silver," (St Matt. xxvi. 15), and they "were glad," and "he promised." (St Luke xxii. 5, 6.)

Little by little Judas had allowed himself to get into Satan's grip. Mortal sin never comes all at once, though to lookers-on it may appear to do so. Satan had been preparing for this a long time—perhaps ever since Judas was called to be an apostle. He had noticed his weak point, and had suggested little infidelities with regard to the money bag—perhaps at first no more than *borrowing* with the full intention of paying back; the next step would be borrowing *and forgetting* to pay back; then borrowing without the slightest intention of paying back; then irritation at money being spent—even on his Master! Little by little Satan had suggested, and Judas had listened; now Satan has taken entire possession of his soul, he can do what he will, suggest even this terrible sin; and to Judas, so skilfully trained in evil, it does not seem much worse than the others. Here is a chance for you of getting money; you have only to say that you will point Him out, you will not do *Him* any harm, for, of course, He will escape again, as He always does.

POINT III.

THE BARGAIN

It is the history of every sin. Sin is a bargain with the devil. What will you *give* me? what shall I get by it? *Something* certainly—"the pleasures of sin for a season," riches, honor, friends, ease, comfort, the gratification of self without any restraint. It is all very attractive, and it is just what I want; but I cannot get it for nothing, what have I to offer? "*I will deliver Him unto you.*" *I* will give *Him* up, turn traitor to my best Friend, give Him away, treat Him as I would not dream of treating an earthly friend, go against His wishes, His commands—to say nothing of hurting His loving Heart and disappointing Him.

It is a sad, a terrible picture; but before I turn away from it, let me just think. Have I never formed a part of that picture? Have I never made this bargain—given up JESUS, and taken instead what Satan handed to me? And as I renew my contrition, let me determine to make greater reparation than ever this Lent.

Colloquy with JESUS

Resolution. To make reparations for those who will deliver up JESUS today.

Spiritual Bouquet. "He that eateth bread with Me shall lift up his heel against Me." (St John xiii. 18.)

— ❧ —

The Preparation of the Pasch

Second Week. Tuesday.

"Where is the guest-chamber where I may eat the Pasch with My disciples?" (St Luke xxii. 11.)

1st *Prelude.*   Peter and John following the man with the pitcher.
2nd *Prelude.*   Grace to aid in the preparation.

POINT I.
"GO AND PREPARE FOR US THE PASCH"

It is already Thursday—*Holy* Thursday—a day so full of precious memories. The Pasch has to be eaten in Jerusalem to-night; and JESUS, having left Bethany for the last time, is wending His way thither with His disciples, saying many wonderful things to them as they walked. They remind Him that today is the first day of the Azymes or unleavened bread, and that the Pasch (the Paschal lamb) has to be killed and prepared. "Where wilt Thou that we go and prepare for Thee to eat the Pasch?" (St Matt. xxvi. 17.) The Master's Eyes rest on Peter and John—faith and love, for He ever needs these when He wants something done for Him: "Go and prepare for us the Pasch that we may eat." But *"where?"* they ask.

Then come the plain directions: "Go into the city, and you will meet a man carrying a pitcher of water; follow him into the house where he entereth in."

"Where wilt Thou that we prepare the Pasch?" How! the question must have struck Him! The Passover Lamb for this particular Feast had been prepared from all eternity. *"Deus providebit sibi victimam holocausti."* God will provide for Himself the Lamb (Gen. xxii. 8), "the lamb without blemish" (Ex. xii, 5). The Lamb of God was preparing to deliver Himself up, even this very night; and He had been trying for some time to prepare the minds of His disciples—trying to make them understand that *He* was the Victim.

"Where wilt Thou that *we* prepare?" I must have a share in that "*we*." Where wilt Thou, Lord, that *I* prepare? In your heart, my child. Accustom yourself to the fact that your Master *is* a Victim, and that, if you will follow Him, you must be a victim too, prepared, and ready to be offered. Lay down your *will* at the foot of My Altar, and then you can say: "O GOD, my heart is ready, my heart is ready."

POINT II.

"WHERE IS THE GUEST-CHAMBER?"

Peter and John were to follow the man with the pitcher into whatever house he entered, and to deliver their message to the Master of the house. "The Master saith: My time is near at hand; where is the guest-chamber where I may eat the Pasch with My disciples?" He is the Master, everything belongs to Him, but He only makes use of His privilege of Ownership when it is necessary. (A lesson for *me* this Lent.) He had need of the ass and colt on Sunday, and His message to their owner was just as simple: "Say ye to him: The Lord hath need of them." That is sufficient.

"My time is near at hand." How touching that He should put that in! Did the master of the house wonder what it meant? Did Peter and John understand how much was contained in their message? To the Master Himself it was all so simple, and He just said what was uppermost in His mind. The time for eating the Pasch is near at hand, but that means that *My* time is near too, My hour is almost come. Where is the guest-chamber? "And he will show you a large dining-room *(cenaculum)* furnished. There prepare."

How happy was that master of the house to be thus singled out and asked to lend a room to Jesus! and unlike the masters of the houses at Bethlehem, thirty-three years before, he did not refuse, but evidently gave his *best* room, for it was "large" and "furnished."

And how happy am I! for does not Jesus send to me, too, a direct message—The Master has need of something, the Master says: "My child, give Me thy heart." Let me see to it that I, too, respond generously and give Him my best—a heart big with love for Him and furnished with all the things that He will expect to find there when He comes.

Point III.

"They found as He had told them"

It is ever so; if we go obediently forward where He sends us, we shall find all straightforward and easy. He does not make promises and fail to fulfil them, nor set impossible tasks, nor send us on fruitless errands. It was, all as He had told them; and when they saw the man with the pitcher, and were so hospitably received by the master of the house, how it must have strengthened their faith and love, and made them feel ready for whatever might lie before them!

My way may seem to be blocked, I may be dreading the difficulties in front of me, but let me only obey Him and trust Him, prepare my heart for Him and for all that He has in store for me, and I shall find all just as He said. He will keep His promises—"Behold, I am with you all the days. Fear not, it is I."

Colloquy with Jesus, my Master.

Resolution. To do *something* today towards the furnishing of my guest-chamber.

Spiritual Bouquet. "Where wilt Thou that *we* prepare?"

The Eating of the Pasch

Second Week. Wednesday.

"And when the hour was come. He sat down, and the twelve Apostles with Him." (St Luke xxii. 14.)

1ˢᵗ *Prelude.* Jesus sitting down with the twelve, and eating the Paschal lamb.
2ⁿᵈ *Prelude.* Grace to take my part in. it all.

Point I.
"One of you"

It is sunset—the hour for eating the Pasch, and Jesus is sitting down with the twelve. "When they were at table eating," a gloom spread over the little company, for their dear Master was troubled in spirit. He soon lets them know why, for He keeps nothing from them: "Amen, I say to you, one of you that eateth with Me shall betray Me!" No wonder He was troubled! One of *you,* of My own chosen ones, who has lived with Me, and worked with Me, whom I have taught and trained and loved, whom I have called not servants but *friends,* from whom I have had no secrets—one of *you* shall betray Me.

I am going to follow Him closely through all the scenes of these last few hours of His life, making myself one of the little company, and so I must ask myself: Is Jesus ever troubled in spirit about *me*? *One* of *you*—if He said this to His own chosen band of Apostles, He can certainly say it to the little world of which I form a part, for it is quite possible for Him to be betrayed still, quite possible for His Own chosen friends to act as if He were not their Friend, not their Master, to return His goodness and love by base acts of which no one suspects them, but which cause Him infinite pain. "One of you shall betray Me." Oh, my Master, never again shall that one be I.

Point II.

"Is it I?"

"They being very much troubled, began *every one* to say: Is it I, Lord?" Should *I* have been humble enough to ask the question? Should I have thought it possible that *I* could be a traitor? "One by one" they ask: "Is it I?" There is no astonishment that their Master could think such things of them, no casting of suspicious looks on their companions; no, each one is absorbed with an intense anxiety to make sure that *he* is not going to betray his Master. "Is it I?" asks Peter. John, leaning on His breast and listening to the Sacred Heart beating with love for him, asks: "Is it I?" Judas, too, asks the question, with what motives who shall say? Perhaps he thought it would arouse suspicion in the minds of the others if he alone kept silent—he seems to have waited till the last. (St Matt. xxvi. 25.) Or perhaps he was not sure yet whether he would carry out his part of the agreement made yesterday at the Sanhedrin's Council. Perhaps he was getting anxious, and wondering how much Jesus knew about it all, and whether He *is* going to escape this time; the Master may answer him (He does not seem to have answered the others) and settle the question one way or the other. And so he asks: "Is it I, Rabbi?"

Point III

"Thou hast said"

Quickly comes the answer, and a very emphatic one, Jesus had said, even before Judas had put the question: "Woe to that man by whom the Son of man shall be betrayed; it were better for him if that man had not been born." (St Matt. xxvi. 24.) What severe words for our loving and long-suffering Master! and how it must have pained Him to say them! He was, in His mercy, giving Judas another chance, and He will still give him others; but Judas is possessed by Satan, and he turns a deaf ear. "Is it I, Rabbi?" he asks abruptly, as though he would say: We both know that it is, and you may as well say so. And the Master whispers the momentous words: *Thou hast said it;* that is: "Thou art the man."

It is all very terrible, and gloom cannot but take possession of our hearts, too, as we meditate about it. The thought *will* come into our minds that there is the possibility of it being said of us: "Better for that one if he had not been born!" And the Master Himself, so full of tender love for us, means us to recognize the possibility, as one of the surest ways of avoiding a verdict so terrible. Let us trust Him and love Him. Let us, with St John, keep ever close to His Sacred Heart, and then even if we do, in moments of weakness, play the traitor, our love will bring us back to Him, and His love will forgive.

Colloquy with the Sacred Heart of Jesus.

Resolution. Not to do wilfully the least thing today that could trouble the Heart of Jesus.

Spiritual Bouquet. "One of you." "Is it I?"

— ⚜ —

JESUS washing His Apostles' Feet

Second Week. Thursday.

"He riseth from supper, and layeth aside His garments, and, having taken a towel, girded Himself." (St John xiii. 4.)

1st *Prelude.*   JESUS washing His Apostles' feet.
2nd *Prelude.*   Grace to learn the wondrous lessons.

POINT I
JESUS THE SERVANT

Before a very great feast it was the custom for a slave to wash the guests' feet. Though the Apostles knew it not, a greater Banquet was about to take place than either the Paschal Supper, or the Social Banquet which had followed it. JESUS loving His own with an eternal love, and with an intense desire to eat this *Last* Supper with them, would show them first the importance of being *"clean"* before partaking of it. And so "when supper (the Social Banquet) was done," (St John xiii. 2), He took off His outer garment, girded Himself with a towel, poured water into a basin, and humbly kneeling before each of His Apostles, He washed not only the feet that were going to carry His Gospel into all the world, but also those which were going to be swift to shed His Blood. "I am in the midst of you as He that serveth," (St Luke xxii. 27)—as the slave! What love, and what humility!

He comes to me, too, and washes my feet in every absolution that I receive. Let me think sometimes of all He had to go through before He could do this—He *humbled* Himself even unto death. And let me remember too that, in the Sacrament of Penance, as in this foreshadowing of it, all turns upon the dispositions of those whose feet are being washed. JESUS, through His representatives, will wash the feet of a

Judas as well as those of a Peter, but if there is no contrition in the heart, their guilt will remain, yea, it will be increased.

Point II
Jesus the Master.

He begins with Peter, and Peter objects: "Lord, *Thou* wash *my* feet?" Then Jesus acts as *the Master,* and tells Peter that he cannot understand His actions now, but that he will understand later. Peter answers with great emphasis, as though he would say: Whether I understand or not, Thou shall *never* wash my feet. Quietly the Master answers His impulsive Apostle: "If I wash thee not, thou hast no part in Me." Peter's point of view is changed in a moment; the thought of having no part in his Master, nothing to do with Him, no share in interests, is far worse than the humiliation of having his feet washed by Him. And so impulsively again he says: "Lord, not only my feet, but also my hands and my head." If it is such a good thing, let me have all I can of it. Patiently, on His knees, the Master waits, while He explains to His impetuous but warm-hearted Apostle the lesson He wanted to teach, not only to St Peter, but to all St Peter's flock—that before receiving Holy Communion, the little defilements (such as are contracted by the feet in walking from the bath) are to be cleansed away too. "He that is *washed* ('*bathed,*' the Greek word means) needeth not but to wash his feet, but is clean wholly." You are in a state of grace, there is no need to wash you wholly, but I want to wash your feet, I want you to have a perfect contrition for all the little defilements that I can see in you, before you receive Me into your heart.

All this Peter did not understand yet, because He did not understand about Holy Communion, but afterwards the lesson would come back to him; and John wrote it down that all might learn it. Have I learnt it? Do I each time before receiving Holy Communion ask our Lord to wash my feet which may have got soiled since I was bathed in His precious Blood at my last Confession, telling Him while He does so how sorry I am?

POINT III.

JESUS THE EXAMPLE

But this was not the only lesson that JESUS meant to teach. He kneeled humbly before each of the others, and, when He had finished, He put on His outer garment, sat down again at the Supper Table, and said to them: "Know you what I have done to you? I have *given you an example,* that as I have done to you, so you do also." If I, your Master, can wash your feet, you can wash one another's; "the servant is not greater than his lord, neither is the apostle greater than He that sent him; if you *know* these things, you shall be blessed if you do them."

Serving others by acts of charity and humility. This is the example the Master has given us to copy, and He presents some sharp contrasts to bring His lessons home—the Master and the servant; the One Who sends and the one sent; the knowledge of charity and humility, and the practice of them.

This example and these lessons are for me. How can I wash the feet of others? By doing little acts of kindness and especially to my inferiors; by taking the lowest place "by esteeming others better than myself"; (Phil. ii. 3); by never seeking my own; (1 Cor. xiii. 5); by taking the worst; and so ensuring that others get the best; by doing what are called *menial* duties, that is, the duties my Master chose to do for me. Every time that I thus put into *practice* the things that I *know,* I not only earn from my Master's lips the title of *blessed,* but I find myself kneeling and washing *His* Feet, those Sacred Feet that were pierced for me, for He says: "As long as you did it to one of these My least brethren, you did it to *Me*." (Matt. xxv. 40. Is it not worth while? And shall I not eagerly seize every opportunity of stooping down to kiss those precious wounds?

Colloquy with JESUS.

Resolution. Not to let today pass without washing His Feet.

Spiritual Bouquet. "You *know* these things, you shall be blessed if you *do* them."

The Last Supper

Second Week. Friday.

"My Flesh is meat indeed, and My Blood is drink indeed. He that eateth My Flesh and drinketh My Blood, abideth in Me, and I in Him," (St John vi. 56, 57.)

1st *Prelude.*   A picture of the Last Supper.
2nd *Prelude.*   Grace to understand more, and to love more.

POINT I.
THE HOLY EUCHARIST AND THE PRIESTHOOD

At the beginning of the Paschal Supper, Our Lord had said: "With desire I have desired to eat this Pasch with you before I suffer"; and perhaps the Apostles had wondered why His desire for this particular Passover Supper was so intense. Now they will see that it was because, after it, He was going to institute the eating of the *New Pasch*. "GOD will provide Himself a Lamb." (Gen. xxii. 8.) And for this blest moment GOD had waited, and the Lamb had waited, from all eternity.

Taking a piece of the unleavened bread that was left on the Supper-table, "He blessed, and broke, and gave to His disciples, and said: *Take ye, and eat. This is My Body.*" It is done. The miracle is worked. JESUS, their Master, is within them. Then—for He must show the *Sacrifice* as well as the Sacrament—"taking the chalice He gave thanks, and gave to them, saying: Drink ye all of this, for this is My Blood of the New Testament, which shall be shed for many unto remission of sins." "And they all drank of it." They all partook of the Sacrifice, How simply was this, the greatest of all the Sacraments, instituted!

But He has not finished yet. He must institute another Sacrament to guard the Holy Eucharist, and to make it possible for Him to say: "Behold, I am with you *all days,* even unto the consummation of the world." A perpetual sacrifice needs a perpetual priesthood, and so He adds the words: "Do *this for a commemoration of Me,*" thereby establishing a new priesthood for the new Pasch—a priesthood that shall have the power to do what He has just done, namely, change bread and wine into His Own most precious Body and Blood.

What marvellous miracles took place in that Guest-chamber! Little did Peter and John guess for what a great Banquet they were preparing. Little did the master of the house guess what honor for all time would rest upon his house when he so generously gave his best room, Little did the Apostles know what wonderful changes would be wrought for them and in them; and little do I know what miraculous changes He will work in my heart if, with faith and love, I offer it to Him as a Guest-chamber, and then let Him do as He will there.

POINT II.
THE DIPPED BREAD

Judas shared all these marvellous privileges, as he had shared in the washing of the feet. He received Holy Communion, and he received the same priestly powers as; the others. The Master would teach us the important lesson that the Sacraments are not charms, and that they have no power *in themselves* to save us. In His mercy, however, He tries to warn Judas through them. He had just said after washing their feet: "You are clean, *but not all.*" And now, as He hands the chalice to the Apostles, He says: "The hand of him that betrayeth Me is with Me on the table." JESUS is still yearning for his soul, and longing to save it.

Peter is getting impatient at all these covered hints that the Master is giving; he wants to *know,* (The "*thou hast said*" was evidently *whispered* to Judas at the Social Banquet, for his companions were still quite in the dark), and he makes signs to John, who was leaning on JESUS breast, to ask the Master who the traitor was. "Lord, who is it?" asks the beloved disciple. And JESUS, unwilling to point out Judas, again answers in a *whisper: "He it is to whom I shall reach bread dipped."* "And when He had dipped the bread, He gave it to Judas Iscariot the son of Simon." It was a sign of special friendship, and He gives it to Judas, trying once again to touch that hardened heart. It had, however, the opposite effect, for "after the morsel Satan entered into him."

POINT III.
NIGHT

JESUS speaks again—speaks to Judas: "*That which thou dost, do quickly.*" Judas alone knew what He meant. The others thought the Master was giving some little direction to him in connection with his work. Not even Peter and John, who now knew who the traitor was, dreamed of anything so sudden. "That thou dost, do quickly"; there is nothing more to wait for, I have done all I have to do, I shall no longer hinder you, nor stand in Satan's way; My hour is come, I am ready. "*And he went out immediately*"—left for ever the little band of which he had formed a part during the last three years. "*And it was night.*" Of course it was! How could it be anything else for one who had turned his back on the Light? It was night in his soul; there was a darkness there that might be felt—the awful darkness of mortal sin. One by one he had deliberately put out all the lights, and now instead of being one of the honored ministers of the Light of the world, he is a slave to the Prince of darkness.

Let me give one look after the faithless Apostle, and remember, for my warning, that his soul was in darkness only because he had put out the lights of grace instead of corresponding to them; and let me think a little about *my* correspondence to the grace and the opportunities offered to *me*.

Colloquy with the Master, Who is always giving me, too, another chance.

Resolution. To be more careful about correspondence to grace.

Spiritual Bouquet. "He went out immediately, and it was night."

— ❦ —

Last Words

Last Words

Second Week. Saturday.

"Little children, yet a little while I am with you." (St John xiii. 33.)

1ˢᵗ Prelude.   Jesus sitting at the Supper table with the eleven.
2ⁿᵈ Prelude.   The grace to treasure His last words.

POINT I.
"WHITHER I GO, YOU CANNOT COME"

A sort of relief seems to have come over the spirit of the Master when Judas had gone. He can say things now, when all are of one mind, that He could not say before. Is my presence ever a hindrance to the things that Jesus wants to say or do?

"Now," He says, *"is the Son of Man glorified, and God is glorified in Him."* What has suddenly brought this glory to the Father and the Son? What but the Institution of the Blessed Sacrament? For now "from the rising of the sun even to the going down (at every hour of the day) My Name will be great among the Gentiles (not only among the Jews), and in every place (all the world over) there shall be sacrifice (the Sacrifice of the Mass), and there shall be offered to My Name a clean Oblation" (the precious Body and Blood of Christ). (Malachias i. 11).

He tells them that the time is very short now, that He is only with them for a little while, that they cannot come with Him yet, but that they shall join Him some day. They have much to learn first; not yet are they ready—though some of them think they are—to follow their Master even unto death. Their will is good, but they must be tested; and they will learn through the humiliation caused by their infidelity, by failing their Master when He most needed them, even by their falls, what it means to be a true disciple. Then they shall follow Him—yes, each one of them—even unto death.

POINT II.

MANY MANSIONS

Seeing gloom again coming over their faces, He says: "Let not your heart be troubled," you have nothing to fear, "in My Father's House are many mansions," there is one there for each of you; I am going to prepare it for you, and I must go alone. *The mine-press must be trodden alone, not a man with Me,* (Isaias lxiii. 3), for no man can understand what the preparation of his place in Heaven costs Me.

For me, too, JESUS has prepared a mansion—an abiding place—in Heaven. Here on earth I am only "as a stranger in the land, and as a wayfaring man turning in to lodge." (Jer. xiv. 8.) "A pilgrim and a stranger on the earth, seeking a better country," (Heb. xi. 13-16), where I know that my place is being prepared. But can I do nothing to help in the preparation? Yes, while JESUS is preparing the place for me, I can be preparing myself for the place, keeping my mind fixed upon it, determined never to let the attractions of the land I am passing through make me forget that it is not my home. A *pilgrim does* not surround himself with comforts and luxuries, he does not seek his ease, nor even stop to rest, more than is absolutely necessary to enable him to continue his journey—it is not worth while, he would rather wait till he gets home. And the *stranger* putting up at the inn for the night, does he throw all his interests into the inn? Is he concerned about the bad taste in the furniture and the ornaments on the mantelpiece? Does the want of refinement at table and in his companions annoy him? Oh no, he scarcely notices these, he is thinking of home and of his place there. *Strangers and Pilgrims on the earth.* This must be true of me, if I am preparing for my place. Let me think often of my Master's last words: "I will come again, and will take you to Myself," when you are ready. How distressed He must be if I love the inn so much that I hardly ever think of home!

POINT III.

A COMMAND AND A LEGACY

(1) *The Command.* "Love one another, as I have loved you." He addresses them very tenderly as "Little children," and tells them that He wants love for one another to be the mark of their discipleship. So this new commandment is for me too, if I count myself as one of His disciples. The love is to be no measured love—not a natural love, just loving those to whom I am attached—no, but "as *I have loved you.*" I know how that was, He loved me when I was a sinner; He loved me enough to give up Heaven, and all He loved best, to save me; He loved me when nobody else could find anything to love in me; He loves me now in spite of all that makes me unlovable; He loves me though I offend Him, and do so much that He does not like; He loves me though oftentimes I do not return His love. And one of His last words is a *command,* love each other as *I have loved you.* I loved *to the end,* do the same, let there be no limit to your love.

(2) *The Legacy.* "Peace I leave with you: My peace I give unto you, not as the world giveth, do I give unto you," Peace, not trouble. *My* peace—the only peace that *is* peace—the peace that I came on earth to bring. I brought it with Me from Heaven, and now I leave it with you, My disciples.

I am one of His disciples; that legacy of peace, then, is for me. Would people guess, if they were not told, that I have had this legacy? Does peace *reign* in my soul, keeping me calm, patient, gentle, forbearing, charitable, silent under provocation and injury and false accusation and misunderstandings? *My* peace—something so great that all these little things on the surface do not touch it. "Would it not be better for me to live down there, in those deep, calm, still waters; instead of on the surface, where every wind that blows has the power to upset me?

> *Colloquy* with JESUS, Who is saying to me: My little child, remember that it is only *a little while,* do not ever be *troubled,* think often of the *place prepared* for you, do not forget that you are a *stranger* and a *pilgrim, love* all as I love you, and draw largely from My legacy of *peace.*

Resolution. To remember His last words.

Spiritual Bouquet. "Let not your heart be troubled."

— ❧ —

His Mother

Third Sunday of Lent.

"A certain woman from the crowd, lifting up her voice, said to Him:Blessed is the womb that bare Thee, and the paps that gave Thee suck. But He said: Yea rather, blessed are they who hear the word of God, and keep it." (The "Gospel.")

1ˢᵗ *Prelude.*   The woman crying out these words.
2ⁿᵈ *Prelude.*   The grace to be amongst the "yea rather, blessed."

POINT I.
"A CERTAIN WOMAN"

We have not met His Mother as yet in our Lent Meditations, but now on this third Sunday the Church brings her to

From the *Campion Missal and Hymnal*

our notice, so we will turn aside, and have a little talk with her about her Son, and about our Lent. We have not far to go when we turn from JESUS to Mary, and we shall not lose anything, nor have the least distraction. On the contrary, we shall find that no one understands better than Mary the spirit of Lent, and that no one is better able than she to help us in our efforts to copy her Son.

JESUS had just finished explaining about the seven devils, who found shelter in the swept and garnished but untenanted house, when His Mother and His brethren appeared on the scene. (St Matt, xii. 46.) Mary, of course, drew no attention to herself; she was quietly waiting for an opportunity to speak to Him, when a certain woman—a *mother* surely—caught sight of her. She had evidently been listening to the Master's discourse, and she gave vent to the admiration she felt, by crying out to the whole multitude the thought that was uppermost in her mind: What a blessed woman must she be who is His Mother! She did not know so much about it all as Elizabeth knew, though she said almost the same thing. She was full of admiration, and enthusiasm, and generosity, mixed, perhaps, with just a tinge of envy; and JESUS was pleased, and Mary was pleased.

Do I please JESUS and Mary by the whole-heartedness with which I say: "Blessed art thou amongst women, and blessed is the Fruit of thy womb JESUS"?

POINT II.

"YEA RATHER, BLESSED"

It is just that tinge of envy that the Master notices, and, in His love, He sees in it a desire for something higher, and He is going to satisfy that desire. Yes, quite right, she is indeed blessed in being My Mother, but she is more blessed still for another reason, namely, that she hears the word of God, and keeps it; and in this you can follow her and be blessed too.

It is to listen to this counsel that I have turned aside today: Blessed are they that hear, and keep God's word, that is, Blessed are the obedient. And who are the obedient? Those who *love*. "If you love Me, keep My Commandments." "My little children, let us not love in word, but in *deed*." (1 John iii. 18.) It brings us back to the point we have reached in our meditations, to the new commandment of love, for all is contained in it. The "Epistle" for today teaches the same lesson. St Paul says: "Be ye followers of God as most dear children, and walk in love, as Christ also hath loved us."

Would I be amongst the *rather blessed*? There is only one way—the way that Mary chose. She gives the directions herself: "Whatsoever He shall say to you, do ye." (St John ii. 5.) These directions can only be followed by those who love, and those who follow them are blessed.

Point III.

The Mother Waiting

They tell Him, at last, that she is waiting to speak to Him. But He is still anxious about those who need His counsel more than she does—about *me,* perhaps—and He says: "Who is My Mother, and who are My brethren? Whosoever shall do the will of My Father Who is in Heaven, he is My brother and sister and mother." I count as My nearest and dearest those whose wills are the most closely united with My Father's. Conformity to God's Will—it was for *this* that I chose My Mother, *this is* why I love her more than all besides, *this* is why I never say "*Nay*" to anything she asks.

Let me wait here with you, my Mother; I am so glad I turned aside. Who, better than yourself, can help me to learn the meaning of conformity to GOD's Will. Teach me to say, as you did: "Behold the handmaid of the Lord," ready to do anything that He asks. You know how difficult it is sometimes; you know what suffering means. Deprivation, mortification, separation, desolation—all are familiar words to you; and they spell the one word, *sanctification*—the word that makes the *Saints*—the *blessed*. I do want to be conformable, I do want to do the Will of my Father. I do want your dear Son to count me as His mother, or sister, or brother. I do want to follow Him in His sufferings, and to go on faithfully to the end of my Lent. Will you come with me? You can take me nearer to Him than I should get by myself, because you are His Mother, and can always gain admission.

Colloquy with His Mother.

Resolution. To aim at conformity to GOD's Will today.

Spiritual Bouquet. "Behold My Mother and My brethren!"

— ❧ —

Warnings

Third Week. Monday.

"And when they had sung a hymn, they went forth to the Mount of Olives." (St Mark xiv. 26.)

1*st* *Prelude.* JESUS and His disciples singing the hymn, as they left the supper table.

2*nd* *Prelude.* Grace to arise and go with them.

POINT I.
"ARISE, LET US GO"

Sweet and precious moments—but they are over now, it is time to leave the Cenacle, They sing the Hymn of

Thanksgiving; the Heart of Jesus is full of joy, because His Hour is come; and the disciples have far more to be thankful for, than as yet they realize. Jesus has still much to say to them, but He will say it on the way to the Mount of Olives. *"Arise, let us go."* There is no flinching, no hesitation, as He starts on His journey to shame, suffering, and death; but He wants His children with Him. "Behold, *we* go up," He said at the beginning of Lent, and now before we are half-way through, He reminds us that we are to have a share: "Let *us* go."

Let me learn from my Master how to meet my crosses, my difficulties and sufferings. When I am inclined to hesitate and put off and be cowardly, let me hear His Voice full of encouragement and joy: Arise, let us (you and me) go to meet the cross. We will go together. "*With me* you can do all things."

Point II.

The Shepherd and the Sheep

As they walk along, Jesus says to them: "*You will all be scandalised in My regard this night.*" This time it was not "*one* of you," but *all*. He means that when they see Him seized and bound, it will be too much for them, and they will all run away. To make His meaning quite clear, He quotes the prophecy about Himself from the prophet Zacharias: "I will strike the Shepherd, and the sheep of the flock shall be dispersed." (Ch. xiii. 7.) He had done His best to make them understand that the Son of Man should be delivered into the hands of His enemies, but He knew that it would come as a shock to them, and that they would be scandalied in Him.

How often has He warned me of the suffering that will surely come to me if I have bound up my life and my interests with His! And yet, when the cross is in sight, it proves so great a shock and surprise, that I say: "This is really too much. I cannot face it. It is more than can be expected of me." In short, I am *scandalized*. The cross —yes, Jesus Himself— proves a stumbling-block. The poor sheep cannot bear the sight of the smitten Shepherd, and it turns and flees! Let me be careful, and take my Master's warning to myself, "You shall *all* be scandalized." It may be that I already need the warning. It may be that I am beginning to think that I was a little too enthusiastic at the beginning of Lent, that there are some of my rules that it would be just as well to relax. It may be that I am beginning to shirk the mortifications and penances that I arranged for myself, with so much care and love, such a little while ago. If so, let me listen to my Master's warning, and remember that the servant must not be above his Master. The Shepherd has been smitten; that is the very reason why the sheep should be smitten too. He was smitten for me. Cannot I bear a little for Him without being scandalized?

Point II.

Peter specially Warned

Peter could not bear to think that he was included in his Master's "*all*," and he answered impetuously: "Though *all* shall be scandalized, *I* will never be." He cannot have meant to imply that he was, in any way, superior to his companions; but he spoke for himself, which was all he could do. His love for his Master was so great that he felt that whatever the others might do, *he* could not be faithless, could not desert Him in His hour of need. Peter was genuine, but he did not know his own weakness, And as he would not be warned by the general warning, but exempted himself from needing it, his Master gave him a special one, telling him that he would be—not better than the others, but—*worse.* "*This night,* before the cock crow twice, thou shalt *deny* Me thrice." Deny Thee! Impossible ! "Though I should die with Thee, I will not deny Thee." He spoke "the more vehemently," St Mark says, and the others all agreed with him.

The Master knows the weaknesses of each one of His children, and in His love He warns them. Peter felt himself above the warning; he was too sure of himself; he lacked humility. Let me take heed. I have had several warnings from my Master already this Lent; have I received them thankfully and humbly? or have I thought myself above them? My love and zeal are not equal to Peter's, and yet *he* fell. "Let him that thinketh himself to stand, take heed lest he fall." (1 Cor. x. 12.)

Colloquy with my Master, Who is warning me.

Resolution. To listen humbly to His warnings.

Spiritual Bouquet. "You will all be scandalized in regard to Me."

— ❧ —

Fruit-bearing

Third Week. Tuesday.

"In this is My Father glorified, that you bring forth very much fruit, and become My disciples." (St John xv. 8.)

1ˢᵗ Prelude. JESUS talking to His disciples, as they walk.
2ⁿᵈ Prelude. Grace to walk with them, and listen.

POINT I.
THE VINE

He talks to them as they walk of fruit-bearing—that necessary outcome of discipleship. He tells them that it is because they are *"clean,"* that He is able to talk to them about this. It is one of the things He waited to say till Judas had gone. It is only those who are free from mortal sin who *can* bring forth fruit. He makes the whole thing clear to them by the figure of the vine: "I am the Vine, you are the branches." If the branches are to bear fruit, they must be a part of the vine." As the branch cannot bear fruit of itself, unless it abide in the vine, so neither can you, unless you abide in Me." The secret of all fruit-bearing is to abide in Christ, to be as entirely a part of Him as the branches are a part of the vine—the sap running from one into the other, their life one, their fruit-bearing one. The closer the union, the better will be the fruit. "He that abideth in Me, and I in him, the same beareth *much* fruit."

Fruit-bearing depends, then, on my union with Christ, that is, on my interior life. The work is done within, not on the surface. The surest way of having a good vintage is not to look scrupulously at each grape and wonder whether it is good enough, but to attend to the stem and the root of the vine, and to be sure that nothing is preventing the life-sustaining sap from reaching the branches. If my "life is hid with Christ in GOD," if the life I am living is no more mine than the life of the vine branches is theirs, if it is Christ Who liveth in me as it is the vine which lives in each branch, then my fruit is assured, I need not trouble. Christ will bear His Own fruit as surely as the vine will bear its own, and in both cases it *is* on the *branches* that the fruit will appear.

POINT II.

THE BRANCHES

The branch, then, has not much to do—it is united to the great *Stem of Jesse* at Baptism, and the fruit will be all right! Not at all. That does not follow either in the natural or the supernatural world. Our Lord speaks of a *Husbandman;* of branches, that *do not bear* fruit—even of those which *cannot;* of branches that are *withered,* and have to be *burned;* of *purging;* of *more fruit;* of *much fruit,* and of *very much fruit.* It is clear, then, that we have not meditated on the whole subject when we have finished with the first Point. Let me try to see further what the Master means to teach me.

1. "Every branch in Me that beareth not fruit, He (the Great Husbandman) will take away." Why is there no fruit? The soul had life given to it at Baptism; the sap went from the great Stem into the little new branch; it began with the same chance as the others, but it took no care of that precious life, it lost its grace; then it cut itself off from the channels of grace, the life-giving sap no longer flowed into it, and as "the branch *cannot* bear fruit *of itself,"* that is, unless it is getting its life from the vine, "so *neither can you unless you abide in Me."* There are two courses open to such a soul: it can, *if it will,* unstop the channels of grace, and let the life once more flow into it; or it can leave things as they are; and when the Husbandman comes, it "will be cast forth as a branch and shall wither, and they shall gather him up and cast him into the fire, and he burneth."

2. Every branch that beareth fruit, He (the Husbandman) will *purge* it, that it may bring forth more fruit." How much in my life that little word *purge* throws light upon! I *am* a disciple, I want—I long—to bear fruit for my Master, and for GOD's glory. The Husbandman knows my desire, and He helps me to realize it by the process of purging. He trims, He prunes, He cuts, He does not spare, His eye is ever on the fruit, and He knows what is best for it. The branch *is* bearing fruit, but He wants *more* fruit. He is glorified, not

by a few little shrivelled grapes which are just enough to show that the branch is not dead, but by *very much fruit.* And this result can only be obtained by purging. It is a painful process, but if I am set on bearing fruit for GOD's glory, I shall not complain. I shall shrink and quiver, doubtless, under the pain; I shall get smaller and more insignificant and less visible as the knife ruthlessly cuts away all my fine leaves. But I shall hide my wounds in those of the True Vine, my life will be hidden in His, I shall be lost in Him. I shall be so deep down in my interior life, that I shall hardly be able to see the fruit up at the top on the poor little pruned branch. But the Master whispers: It is all right, my child, there is *very much fruit* and *My Father is glorified,* and it is all because the branch was stripped bare, and gave all it had for the sake of the fruit.

POINT III.

THE RESULT

"If you abide in Me, and My words abide in you, you shall ask *whatever you will,* and it shall be done unto you."

To the demands of a soul that abides in Him, and is bringing forth fruit to His Father's glory, our Lord sets no limit. He can trust it, it will do nothing apart from Him, it is a very part of Himself. It cannot have any will or any desires apart from *His* will and *His* desires, It regards everything from His point of view. So when He says: "You shall ask whatever you will," He is quite safe. He is running no risk. He knows that that soul will only ask for what *He* wills, and so, naturally. He adds: "it shall be done unto you." His promise is only another way of saying, that the soul that abides in Him has all that it wants, because it never wants anything that He does not give. The love, and the union, and the mutual understanding are so perfect, that it would be superfluous to ask for anything; every least want is forestalled. What *could* such a soul want more!

Colloquy with the *True Vine.*

Resolution. To be content with nothing less than very much fruit.

Spiritual Bouquet. "*Abide in Me, and I in you.*"

Our Lord's Prayer for His Disciples

Third Week. Wednesday.

"*These things Jesus spoke: and lifting up His eyes to Heaven, He said: Father, the how is come. Glorify Thy Son, that Thy Son may glorify Thee.*" (St John xvii. 1.)

1st *Prelude.*   JESUS praying to His Father, for His disciples.
2nd *Prelude.*   To listen carefully; for His prayer concerns me.

POINT I.
HE COMMENDS THEM TO HIS FATHER

He had said many difficult things to them, many heart-searching things, many disquieting as well as many consoling things. He had put before them a very high standard; and now His hour is come and He must leave them alone. His "*little Flock*" that He has cared for so tenderly—how will it get on without its Shepherd? What can He do to protect it and provide for it? He will explain to His Father all about it, and commend it to His care. And so the last words that the Apostles hear from their Master's lips are a prayer for them—telling His Father all about them, how much He loves them, what He has done for them, and what He wants for them; words which must have shown them, better than anything else could, what the relationship between Him and His Father was. "*I have finished the work Thou gavest Me to do. I have manifested Thy Name to the men whom Thou hast given Me out of the world,*" They know that the words I have spoken to them are *Thy* words, and they have kept them, and they believe now that Thou didst send Me. These are the men for whom I am going to pray; they are Thine, for it was Thyself Who gave them to Me; besides, all My things are Thine, and Thine are Mine. I am not to be in the world any longer, but these *are* in the world. I have sent them there, just as Thou didst send Me. The world hates them because they are not *of it*. While I was with them, *I* kept them, and now I come to Thee to ask Thee to keep them.

How lovingly He introduces His little flock to His Father! And what could have been more consoling to them in the midst of their sorrow and anxiety than to hear these words! What a strength it will be to them in days to come, in the midst of all their difficulties, to recall this wonderful prayer, in which their Master had explained their whole position to His Father, and put them into His keeping.

"*We have an Advocate with the Father, Jesus Christ, the Just.*" (1 St John ii. 1.) What He did on the last day of His life for His Apostles He is ever doing for me, for He "*always liveth* to make intercession for us." (Heb.vii.25.)

POINT II.
WHAT HE PRAYS FOR

(1) For *fidelity.* "Holy Father, keep them in Thy Name." They cannot keep faithful to all I have taught them, and to the commission I have given them, unless Thou dost keep them.

(2) For *unity.* "That they may be one, as we are." All depends upon this unity, and it can never be sustained by *human* hands. So I pray that Thou wouldest keep it in *Thy* Hands. Let it be the closest possible union—*one, as we are.*

(3) For *purity of heart.* "That Thou shouldst keep them from evil." I do not ask for them to be taken out of the world, but to be kept from the evil in the world. I have told them that they will have *distress* in it, but I have told them also that I have *overcome* it. (Ch. xvi. 33.)

(4) For *sanctification*—that great work about which I am so anxious, and about which I have said so much to them. Holy Father, *sanctify* them in Thy truth—make them holy, make them saints.

(5) For *Final Perseverance.* "I will that where I am, they also may be with Me." *I will* that not one of them shall be lost. I have promised them that no man shall pluck them out of My hand, (Ch. x. 28), and that no man shall pluck them out of My Father's hand. I have told them that the Father Himself loveth them because they love Me; (Ch. xvi. 27); and so, "Holy Father, keep in Thy Name those whom Thou hast given Me."

How fully were all these petitions granted! "Him the Father heareth *always.*" Do I believe it?

Point III
"Not for them only do I pray,

but for them also who, through their word, shall believe in Me "—that is, for His Church. And He makes petitions for her which are to last through all the ages. He puts *unity* first as being of such great importance, and He gives the reason for its importance—"That they *all* may be one, *that the world*

may believe that Thou hast sent Me." He is thinking of the
world now, and of the Church's mission in it. He wants the
world to be saved, and He knows that sooner or later it will
be the *oneness* of the Church that will strike and attract it,
and prove to it that the Church is no human institution,
Again He prays *that the world may know that Thou hast loved
them.* He is going to die for the world, and He longs for it to
know of His Father's love. "Just Father, the world hath not
known Thee, but I have known Thee, and these have known
that Thou hast sent Me, and I have made known Thy Name to
them." The plans are all made, the way is open for the world's
salvation. And now. Father, "I will that they may all be with
Me and see My glory." So He prays for His Church and for
the world.

I, as a member of His Church, am included in His petitions. Is it not something for me to know that He thought of
me on His last day on earth, that He prayed to His Father that
I might be made perfect, that I might know that GOD loved
me and sent His Son for me, that GOD's love might dwell in
me, that I might be with JESUS where He is, and might one
day see His glory? In my times of darkness and weariness let
me dwell on each of these petitions; all I can possibly want
is contained in them; and let me remember: "*Him the Father
heareth always.*"

Colloquy with my Master, and with His Father.

Resolution. To refer to this Prayer in my times of
desolation.

Spiritual Bouquet. He is "always living to make intercession for us."

— ❧ —

Gethsemani

Third Week. Thursday.

"He began to fear, and to be heavy, and He saith to them: My soul is sorrowful, even unto death." (St Mark xiv. 33, 34.)

1ˢᵗ Prelude.   A picture of the Agony in the Garden.
2ⁿᵈ Prelude.   Grace to stay with Him and watch.

POINT I.
ENTERING INTO THE GARDEN

They arrive at Gethsemani—JESUS and the Eleven. The word Gethsemani means an *oil-press.* St Matthew calls it "a country place"; St Mark, "a farm"; and St John, "a garden." It is in this enclosed plantation of olive-trees that God's Anointed is going to begin His Passion. It begins in His *Soul.* "My soul is sorrowful," He says, as He enters the garden. "I have trodden the wine-press alone . . . I have stained all my apparel." (Isaias lxiii. 3.)

Before meditating on Our Blessed Lord's bodily sufferings, we must give this one meditation to the sufferings of His *Soul.* The Agony in the Garden was the first Act of the Drama of the Passion, and it was played throughout in His Soul. It was the human Soul of JESUS that was suffering, and by an act of His Will, He withdrew from It even the sensible support of the Divinity. "I have trodden the wine-press *alone."*

He leaves eight of the disciples behind, saying to them: "Sit you here, till I go yonder and *pray."* His mental prayer has already begun, the three powers of His Soul are at work. He allows His three chosen ones to go with Him; they will not disturb Him, He is too much absorbed in prayer; and they will be some consolation. Then by an act of His *Will* the Agony ("*wrestling*" the word means) begins. "He began to fear and to be heavy." It was as though He said to the powers of darkness: You can begin now, I am ready. The words, used to describe His sensations, are very strong in the Greek: that used for *"fear"* is translated elsewhere in St Mark's Gospel "astonished and struck with fear," (ch. ix. 14), and "astonished and affrighted." (ch. xvi. 5, 6). It means *awestruck, amazed.* And the word used for *"to be heavy"* has a far deeper meaning than appears on the surface. It means having so much to bear, that a sensation of giddiness and sickness is produced; it denotes a want of calm and self-possession; it is to be beside one's self, to be on the verge of an unhinging of the mind. This is the state that Our Blessed Lord *allowed* to possess His Soul. "He *began* to be heavy" when the hour had come. "Fear and trembling are come upon me, and darkness hath covered me." (Ps. liv. 6.)

What was it that thus amazed and astonished Him, and filled Him with awe? What was it that made Him sick with fear and apprehension? It was the strangeness of the situation, the dread of something unknown—of some unknown horror. It was not merely the vision of sin; that was not unknown; Our Lord knew all about sin, every form and kind of it; but it was the vision of sin *in contact with Himself.* This He knew nothing about; He had never experienced it; this was the new situation which lay before Him. "The Lord hath laid on Him the iniquity of us all." (Isaias liii. 6.) "His own self bore our sins." (1 Pet. ii. 24.) These words are about to be realized; and His Father's Face is going to be averted in consequence. The powers of Our Blessed Lord's Soul were *perfect,* and as He applied His *understanding* to this point of His mental prayer, His Soul was filled to overflowing with horror and apprehension.

"My Soul is exceedingly sorrowful, even unto death. Stay you here," He says to His three Apostles. And I must stay with them, I cannot go with Him; He must tread the wine-press of GOD's anger *alone*. Sinner that I am, I cannot sympathise, for I cannot understand this horror caused by contact with sin. For me, alas! it is no unknown situation, no new experience. But as I watch Him going alone to the awful conflict, I can do as He bids —watch with Him. I can ask Him to give me a horror of sin, and I can spend the time in contrition, and love and gratitude, as I try to realize something of the sufferings that contact with *my* sin caused His pure and holy Soul.

POINT II.
THE PRAYER AND THE AGONY

He is alone now—alone with His mental agony. Another power of His Soul is at work; His memory is busy recalling all the sins that ever have been, and that ever will be committed in the world. Each one of them is already in contact with His Soul. His Father is already averting His Face. His mental prayer gives place to vocal: "Father, if it be possible, let this chalice pass"—this chalice of suffering which His Father is holding before Him, and which is infinitely worse than any of His bodily sufferings which are to come. It is not of these that He is thinking; they are as nothing in comparison with what His Soul is suffering. "If it be possible, let it pass." But it was not possible. The only way for the Father's justice to be satisfied is for His Son to be *"made sin* for us," (2 Cor. v. 21), and thus to expiate our sin. "Yet, not my will, but Thine be done." It is His Father's Will that He should drink the chalice, and, therefore, it is His Will too. Twice He gets up from His position, prostrate on the ground, and interrupts His prayer to go back and rouse His sleeping Apostles—as though He were afraid to be alone. Again and again He prays "in the self-same words." So great was the mental struggle—the agony of soul—that, from every pore of His skin, the Precious Blood oozed forth and dripped on to the ground, as though it were in a hurry to cleanse away the loathsome thing which, when leave was given, had been so ready to approach.

And, as His agony increased, He prayed the more ardently —prayed as a criminal, as a sinner, as a Penitent; making Acts of Contrition and of Submission to the Will of GOD, such as would never be made even by the greatest of His Saints.

From the *Campion Missal and Hymnal*

POINT III.
THE ANGEL AND THE APOSTLES

It was over at last, Heaven's gates were opened, "and there appeared to Him an Angel from Heaven strengthening Him." He could have had "twelve legions of Angels," if He had permitted them to come. They were longing to help Him, and anxiously waiting to do His bidding, but permission was only given to *one*. What was the Heavenly Consolation that His Father sent Him? The Saints tell us that the privileged Angel brought another chalice, containing the fruits of His awful agony. He saw there countless millions of souls, who, because He had submitted His Will to his Father's, and had allowed their sins to be "laid upon Him," would fulfil the end for which they were created, and glorify GOD through all eternity.

Some of the bitterness in the Chalice of Suffering I know was contributed by me. Let me make sure, as I watch with Him today, that some of the ingredients in the Angel's Chalice of Consolation are contributed by me too.

As Our Blessed Lord goes back to His Apostles for the third and last time, He says to them, with a kind of gentle irony: Sleep on now, and take your rest; I shall not interrupt you any more; the time is gone now. They had failed Him, they could not watch even one hour with Him. It was sorrow and heaviness of heart that made them sleep, no doubt, for the things He had said to them at the Supper-table and since, had filled their hearts with sorrow. "They knew not what to answer Him," they would not excuse themselves. But He, like Himself, makes excuses for them: The spirit is willing, but the flesh is weak; it is enough, the hour is come, behold, he that betrayeth Me is at hand; rise up, let us go. And, strengthened by His conflict, He goes forth to meet treachery, torture and death.

No one knows so well as Thyself, my JESUS, how often I have failed Thee, how often when Thou hast looked for consolation Thou hast found none! Before I rise up to go with Thee through all that Thou hast still to suffer, I want to promise Thee here in this Garden of Thine Agony, that I will watch and pray that I enter not into temptation.

Colloquy with JESUS agonizing for me.

Resolution. To add something today to the Chalice of Consolation.

Spiritual Bouquet. "The Chalice which my Father hath given Me."

— ❧ —

Jesus before Caiaphas

"He was offered because it was His own Will, and He opened, not His mouth." (Isaias liii. 7.)

1*ˢᵗ Prelude.*   The house of Caiaphas.
2*ⁿᵈ Prelude.*   The grace to stand by, and learn the lessons.

After His Prayer and Agony in the Garden, Jesus was betrayed with a kiss, bound, and led away to Annas. (St John xviii. 13.) After a mock trial before him, He was sent to the palace of Caiaphas, where He was tried during the night. This trial, which probably took place at about one o'clock in the morning, is the first of the events of that Great Day on which the world's salvation was wrought. After it Jesus was put into prison, where He was mocked and insulted by the guards till the morning was come and the Sanhedrin could hold its formal council.

Point I.
Jesus is Silent

It is night, and He is alone with His enemies—the ancients, the chief priests, and the scribes—all are there; but no friends—they have all deserted Him. A difficulty presents itself at the outset; they can find no one to witness against the Prisoner! They are obliged to fall back upon *false* witnesses; but these could not agree! At last two came, who brought up what He had said about being able to destroy God's temple, and build it up again in three days—words, the meaning of which they knew nothing. Jesus says nothing, gives no explanation, makes no defence. Let me ask for grace to remember this *in time* when next I am accused, be it justly or unjustly.

Caiaphas is angered by His silence, and standing up threateningly (the soldiers armed with thongs and whips were only waiting for a signal to begin their work), he says: "Answerest Thou nothing to the things that are laid to Thy charge by these men?" But "*He held His peace, and answered nothing.*"

"There is a time to keep silence." (Eccl. iii. 7.) Have I learnt yet what that time is? How often I long just to say the word that will throw light—a different light—on something that I have done. Shall I say it or not? There is an infallible rule which will help me to find out whether silence, which is nearly always best, is best in a particular instance, and that is, to ask myself: *Who will suffer if I keep silence?* If I find that somebody will, I may speak and give the explanation; but if that somebody is only *myself,* I may safely imitate my Master and say nothing. This is not an easy thing to do, and to some natures it is extremely hard; but afterwards there is peace in the heart, and even joy, put there by the Master Himself, Who is glad that in a position, bearing a little resemblance to His, before Caiaphas, His child, out of love to Him, has kept silent and answered nothing.

POINT II.

JESUS SPEAKS

The situation is entirely altered by Caiaphas' next demand: "I adjure Thee by the living GOD that Thou *tell me if Thou be the Christ the Son of GOD.*" It is not silence now that will bring suffering; silence, on the contrary, would be a way of escape. JESUS, though He knows that His answer will cost Him His life, answers calmly:

"*I am;* and hereafter you (you, Caiaphas, and all you Ancients, High Priests and Scribes) shall see the Son of Man sitting on the right hand of the power of GOD and coming in the clouds of Heaven." JESUS here gives the Sanhedrin its chance—it hears from His Own lips the great truths that He is indeed the Son of GOD, and that one day they shall see Him, not standing as a criminal to be *judged by them,* but sitting at GOD's right hand to *judge them.*

"A time to speak." (Eccl. iii. 7.) Let me learn this lesson, too, as I listen to the trial before Caiaphas. Keeping silence under accusation does not mean withholding the truth. I must always speak calmly and fearlessly in the interests of truth, even though I know that I shall suffer for it. And I must, as my Master did, use any opportunity I may get of witnessing a good confession before His enemies.

POINT III.

JESUS IS CONDEMNED TO DEATH

Caiaphas, rending his garments, turns to the assembled; elders and says: "You have heard His blasphemy, what think you?" And they all condemn Him to be guilty of death; for blasphemy, according to the Jewish law, was a capital offence.

It is time now for rest; and while His judges retire for the night, JESUS is left in the Guard-room, where every a kind of insult is shown Him by the guards and servants.

As soon as it is day, the whole Sanhedrin assembles to ratify the sentence passed in the night, for, as Night Councils were illegal, it was invalid. It is quickly done, for they are all of one mind. They pass the sentence that He is *guilty* of death, but further than this they cannot go, for the Romans had deprived them of the power of passing the sentence of death. This could only be done by Pilate. And so "the whole multitude of them rising up led Him to Pilate"—to the Governor's Hall, on the other side of the town.

I will join that Procession; He shall have at least one friend near Him on His painful journey. He is a condemned criminal now, walking in chains, and closely guarded. The things He feared most are all being quickly realized. His own people are on their way to hand Him over to the Gentiles. Oh, my JESUS, Thou didst suffer all this *for me*, because Thou lovest me. As I walk by Thy side, I will never weary of telling Thee how much I love Thee, and I will prove my love—at least today—by bearing patiently all that Thou dost permit to happen to me.

Colloquy with JESUS led through the streets of Jerusalem as a criminal.

Resolution. To accompany Him today.

Spiritual Bouquet. "A time to keep silence, and a time to speak."

— ❧ —

Peter's Denial

Third Week. Saturday.

"Amen, I say to thee, that in this night, before the cock crow, thou wilt deny Me thrice." (St Matt. xxvi. 34.)

1st *Prelude.*   Peter standing amongst the High Priest's servants, warming himself at the fire.

2nd *Prelude.*   Grace to avoid the occasions of sin.

POINT I.
PETER'S FALL

While JESUS was being tried before Annas and Caiaphas, what were His Apostles doing? We saw them last in the Garden with Him; but as soon as they saw the chains put on, "they all forsook Him and fled!" Peter and John, however, came back; they could not bear the thought of leaving their Master in the hands of His foes. John, because he was known to Caiaphas, was allowed into the Court during the trial. Peter, as John's friend, could probably have got in too, had he wished; but he preferred to stay in the "Court below," (St Mark xiv, 66), determined, if possible, to see what happened, without running too great a risk. At first he "stood at the door without," (St John xviii. 16), but John sent a portress to ask him to come and wait inside. As he sat there in the firelight, the portress looked "earnestly" at him, (St Luke xxii. 56), and then asked: "Art not thou also (thou as well as John) one of this Man's disciples?" It was a very natural question; but Peter *denied*, and said: "I am not; I neither know nor understand what thou sayest." (St Mark xiv. 68.) "After a little while," (St Luke xxii. 58), he tried to slip out, thinking to avoid further observation, "but as he went out of the gate another maid saw him," (St Matt. xxvi. 71), and "said to the standers by": (St Mark xiv. 69): "This man also was with JESUS of Nazareth." One of the by-standers charged him with it: "Thou also art one of them." But Peter said: "O man, I am not;" (St Luke xxii. 58); and St Matthew tells us that this second time he denied "with an oath." An hour later (St Luke xxii. 59) Peter was still sitting by the fire "warming himself," (St John mentions this fact *twice),* and his Master was still in the Guard-room, enduring cruel insults, and thinking of Peter. It seemed strange to see one of the Prisoner's friends making himself at home amongst the servants and ministers of His judges! and "they that stood by said: Surely thou art one of them; even thy speech discovers thee to be a Galilean." (St Matt. xxvi. 73.) And the kinsman of Malchus added: "Did not I see thee in the Garden with Him?" (St John xviii. 26.) Then Peter "began to curse and swear, saying: I know not this

Man, of whom you speak." (St Mark xiv. 71.) "And immediately, as he was yet speaking, the cock crew." (St Luke xxii. 6O.) At that same moment JESUS was being led out of the Guard-room to His second trial before Caiaphas.

"And the Lord, turning, looked on Peter . . ."

"And Peter remembered . . . "

"And Peter, going out, wept bitterly."

POINT II.

THE STEPS WHICH LED TO HIS FALL

(1) *Boasting.* "Although all shall be scandalized in Thee, I will never be scandalized."

(2) *Refusing to believe* it possible that he could deny his Master: "Yea, though I should die with Thee, I will not deny Thee."

(3) *Neglecting* to watch and pray.

(4) *Sleeping,* in spite of a special warning to himself: Simon, sleepest *thou;* couldest not *thou* watch? "

(5) *Deserting* His Master at the first sign of danger.

(6) *Following* Him *afar off.*

Are not these the steps that lead to my falls too? If I look back after a fall, I shall generally find one or other of them in the background. *Self-assurance,* thinking *I* am quite safe whatever others may be; *pride,* which prevents me from thinking it possible for *me* to fall; *neglect* of spiritual duties and of little practices that have been recommended to me as a safeguard; *disregard* of special warnings that were given me, and of which I perfectly understood the meaning; letting my soul *sleep* instead of rising to effort; *cowardice* with regard to mortification and penance; and lastly, *following afar off* instead of closely, that is, allowing other things and people to get between me and my Master, and to spoil that union of heart with Him which alone can ensure my safety. Let me make a self-examination on these points, and it may help me not to grieve my Master by a fall again this Lent.

Point III.

The Occasions of the Fall

(1) Peter hesitated. He did not know whether to follow or not; he ran away, came back, followed, stood at the door without, came into the Court below, sat by the fire, then got up and stood. And all the time he might have been inside with John, and been a comfort to his Master!

(2) He deliberately put himself into an occasion of by mingling with the enemies of his Master.

(3) He sought his own comfort—warmed himself by the fire "because it was cold." Was not his Master cold too?

(4) He remained in the occasion of sin after he had fallen once.

Again let me examine myself as to the occasions of my falls. Have I learnt yet that to hesitate is to lose? that prompt, decisive action is the only safe method? Am I careful about occasions of sin, avoiding them as I would a hovel where fever has been? Do I understand how much a general and constant spirit of self-denial helps, when I am face to face with temptation?

Peter loved his Master sincerely; but he relied too much on his own will and strength, and he deliberately allowed his will to be weakened. And so he fell. Two things will safeguard me against yielding in times of temptation;

(1) a firm belief in my power—"*I can do all things in* Him Who strengtheneth me"; (Phil. iv. 13); (2) a firm belief in my weakness—"Without Me *you can do nothing*," (John xv. 5.) With these two weapons—my *strength* and my *weakness*—I

need have no fear. Peter went into battle unarmed, and his fall is for my warning.

> *Colloquy* with Him Who is always ready to be strength in the battle against sin.
>
> *Resolution.* Never to forget my weakness.
>
> *Spiritual Bouquet.* "Power is made perfect infirmity." (2 Cor. xii. 9.)

— ❦ —

Lætare!

Fourth Sunday of Lent.

"Rejoice exceedingly, you who have been in sorrow, . . . leap for joy, and be satiated with comfort." (The "Introit.")

1ˢᵗ Prelude. High Mass today—the Rose-coloured vestments—the organ allowed to speak just once again.

2ⁿᵈ Prelude. The grace to enter into the spirit of the Church.

REJOICE !

Joy is the Church's note today. "Rejoice *exceedingly*," is her command. We have got to the middle of Lent (Thursday was *Mid-Lent,* but the Church reserves her joy for a Festa), and our faces are turned in the direction of the great Festival for which we are preparing. As we peer through the gloom that we have still to traverse, we can almost see the dawn of the Easter day. The Church would have our faith become sight, and so she says: Stand still, look ahead, and *rejoice.*

The whole of the Mass for *Lætare* Sunday breathes forth the spirit of joy and refreshment. By meditating on it, we shall find out how the Church wants her children to rejoice.

(1) *The "Introit."* "Rejoice exceedingly, you who have been in sorrow," you who, out of love for your suffering Lord, have been doing Penance, saying: *"No"* to yourself in hundreds of little ways, known only to Him "Who seeth in secret." Have I brought consolation to the Heart of JESUS this Lent by my efforts for Him? If so, the Church says you may pull up today, and give yourself to rejoicing for all that the grace of GOD has done in you. "Leap for joy, and be satiated with comfort." Enter into the Heart of JESUS, and see His consolation, and rejoice that you have helped to give it.

(2) *The "Collect."* "Grant that we who have been justly afflicted, may *breathe again* by the consolation of Thy grace." *Respiremus*—Let us take a deep breath! So says the Church to her children. Stand still in the middle of the hill, give yourself a little breathing space before you climb the last and the steepest bit. As I stand midway, looking back and looking forward, let me enjoy to the full the refreshment given me; let me open my mouth wide to receive all the inspirations of grace by which I am surrounded. Let me put myself more and more under the direction of the Holy Spirit, Who will breathe into me the breath of life, renewing my strength so that I shall "take wings as eagles, shall run and not be weary, shall walk and not faint." (Isaias xl. 31.)

(3) *The "Epistle"* speaks of bondage being over, and freedom at hand. We are to think of "the freedom wherewith Christ has made us free," and to rejoice at the thought. We are *not* in bondage, whatever the world may say. If we have bonds, it is because we have put them on voluntarily, out of love for Him, Who was bound for us; and they are a sign that we infinitely prefer being the slaves of JESUS Christ to being the world's free-men. To serve Him is perfect freedom. *"Rejoice"* says the "Epistle," for "we are the children of the promise, free from all our sins, our debt paid, happy slaves

wearing the sweet yoke and carrying the light burdens of our great Deliverer."

(4) The "Gradual." "I rejoiced at the things that were said to me." And these things were about *peace* and *abundance* in the House of the Lord. The Church here has a word for those of her children who are beginning to be "weary of their journey." (Numb. xxi. 4.) Look on, she says, the end is not far, do not give up because the journey is hard and full of difficulties, think of the peace and the abundance of GOD's House, and *rejoice* —yea, rejoice that you are counted worthy to suffer.

(5) The "Gospel." Here it is JESUS Himself Who speaks, and His Voice is full of tender sympathy for those who are suffering because they have followed Him so closely. "Make the men sit down," He says, and they sat down on the green grass, while He Himself supplied all their needs with His own Hands. "This is of a truth the Prophet that is to come," they say. And we, too, say:

This is indeed our JESUS, He Who is coming at Easter to make our hearts rejoice. He is giving us a little foretaste today, and dealing out to each just such refreshment and encouragement as he needs, filling our hearts with joy and love, and making us more than ever determined to stay with Him to the end, cost what it may.

(6) In the "Offertory," the Church would have us give our-selves up to praising GOD for His goodness. "He is good: sing ye to His Name, for He is sweet." As our joy is all to be *in Him*, it is only natural that we should spend our time of relaxation in praising Him.

(7) In the "Secret" we ask for an "increase of devotion." We need it to enable us to persevere and to finish our course *with joy*. (Acts xx. 24, Greek.)

(8) In *the* "*Communion*" and "*Postcommunion*" our thoughts are turned towards Jerusalem, whither the tribes went up to praise GOD; and we are reminded of the New Jerusalem whither we are tending. There, nourished by "the holy mysteries with which Thou daily feedest us," we shall sit down one day at the Banquet, which Thou hast prepared for all those who have faithfully passed through earth's trials and tribulations. "Blessed is the man that endureth temptation: for when he hath been proved, he shall receive the crown of life which GOD hath promised to them that love Him." (James i. 12.) Is it not worth while? *Can* the suffering be compared with the glory? No, St Paul says, it is *not worthy.* (Rom. viii. 18.)

Colloquy. I thank Thee, my JESUS, for finding time in the midst of all Thy sufferings to think of me, and to put fresh heart and joy into me. It makes me feel ashamed that I have done so little, but with the joy-bells of Thy words of consolation and encouragement ringing in my ears, I will go on treading faithfully every step of the journey with Thee, and seeing to it that all I do is done out of love to Thee.

Resolution. To finish my course—that is, do all that I planned to do—*with joy.*

Spiritual Bouquet. *Lætare!*

— ❊ —

Peter's Repentance

Fourth Week. Monday.

"And the Lord, turning, looked on Peter. And Peter remembered the word of the Lord, as He had said: Before the cock crow, thou shalt deny Me thrice. And Peter, going out, wept Bitterly." .(St Luke xxii. 61, 62.)

1st *Prelude.* Jesus turning to look.

1ˢᵗ Prelude. Jesus turning to look.
2ⁿᵈ Prelude. Grace to know something experimentally of Peter's repentance.

Point I.
"And the Lord, turning, looked on Peter"

Just as Peter with oaths and curses on his tongue—that tongue which had so recently been consecrated by receiving the Body and Blood of his Lord—was hotly denying that he had any dealings whatsoever with his Master, Jesus was being led from the Guard-room for the morning trial before Caiaphas. He has heard all—every oath, every curse, every denial— and as He passes through the Court below, He deliberately *turns*—an action which is all the more noticeable because He is bound, (St Mark xv. 1)—and looks across towards the fire—*looks on Peter.* And at this same moment the cock crows, and Peter hears it, and remembers the words said to him in the Supper-room the night before: "Before the cock crow, thou shall deny me thrice."

The picture is a sad one, and makes us inclined to weep every time we look at it, whether we think of the Master's side of the question or of the disciple's. But let me be practical and bring the Meditation home to myself. Do not I know well enough that look of Jesus, whether He gives it through one of His representatives, or more directly still through my own conscience; that look, though it may be only momentary, which pierces between the joints of the fine armour of self, "reaches unto the division of the soul and the spirit, of the joints also and the marrow: and is a discerner of the thoughts and intents of the heart," (Heb. iv. 12), making me see myself just for a moment as He sees me. What have I done with these looks which I have so often felt turned upon me after my moments of unfaithfulness? Have I tried to forget them? Have I shrunk from meeting those kind, but sad, eyes? Or have I, like St Peter, let them do their work in my soul? Once He said: "I *looked* for one that would *grieve,* but there was none." (Ps. lxviii. 21.) If He has ever looked in vain for grief and contrition in me, let me try to make reparation this Lent.

POINT II.

"AND PETER REMEMBERED"

In that bitter, yet sweet, moment he remembered all; everything rushed into his mind like a flash. He remembered that it was *His Master* Who had been betrayed, handed over to His enemies, tried, found guilty of death, and that He was now on His way to have the illegal sentence ratified. He remembered His Master's words to him: Before the cock crow, thou shalt thrice deny Me; the cock was now crowing, and he *had* denied Him, yes, three times. He remembered his Master's warning at the supper table, and how he had protested, how sure of himself he had been. He remembered the Garden, and his Master's distress and agony, and His special appeal to *him* not to sleep. He remembered his Communion; he remembered the honor his Master had shown him, by saying to him: "*Do this* in commemoration of Me." He remembered how his Master had washed his feet and had said: "You are clean." (He could not say that now!) He remembered how he had been chosen by his Master to prepare that greatest of all Passover Suppers. Yes, Peter remembered every detail; he read them all at a glance in the eyes of his Master.

And do not *I* remember, too, when Jesus looks at me after a fall? My Communion so recent, fresh responsibilities just given, new work entrusted to me—perhaps just after a Retreat, perhaps in Lent—even in Holy Week, just when I thought I was so near to my Master, and was beginning to feel a little bit sure of myself? How one thing after another rises up to condemn me, and to make my infidelity bigger and bigger in my eyes, till I am afraid of it, and it seems more than I can bear! Only one thing can make it bearable—to do as Peter did, let that *look* of Jesus melt me to contrition.

Point III.

"And Peter, going out, wept bitterly"

He has no more taste for sin now, he leaves the occasion, he has seen things as they are, seen himself as his Master sees him. One thought only fills his big, generous, loving heart—I have grieved Him, and "going out, he *began to weep.*" (St Mark xiv. 72.) He never stopped. St Clement, who succeeded to the Papal Chair some ten years after St Peter's martyrdom, writes that each night when he heard the cock crow, Peter would throw himself on his knees and burst into floods of tears. Ah, Peter's remembrance was not just a passing thought. His Master forgave and forgot, and reinstated him in his office, but Peter could never forgive himself. Peter remembered always; and in his first sermon, preached not many weeks after, his note is *penance:* "Do penance, and be baptized every one of you in the Name of Jesus Christ, for the remission of your sins." (Acts ii. 38.)

I sin—perhaps often—as Peter sinned—but do I repent as Peter did? do I flee once and for all the occasions of my sin?

Am I not a little inclined to remember just long enough to be sorry and to get absolution, and then to go on much the same as before? It is quite true that the thought of past sin should never be allowed to discourage us, nor to hinder us on our journey; but the remembrance of it should always be there, as a kind of background, making gratitude, love, contrition, and reparation stand out more clearly.

> *Colloquy* with JESUS, remembering that it is possible to give Him more consolation by my contrition, than I have given Him pain by my sin.
>
> *Resolution.* To try to increase my contrition this Lent.
>
> *Spiritual Bouquet.* "Felix culpa!"

"He that was called Judas"

Fourth Week. Tuesday.

"Then Judas, who betrayed Him, seeing that He was condemned, repenting himself, brought back the thirty pieces of silver to the chief priests and ancients, saying: I have sinned in betraying innocent blood. But they said; What is that to us? Look thou to it. And casting down the pieces of silver in the temple, he departed, and went and hanged himself with an halter." (St Matt. xxvii. 3-5.)

> 1ˢᵗ *Prelude.* Judas standing again before the chief priests,
> 2ⁿᵈ *Prelude.* The grace to take warning.

POINT I.
"SEEING THAT HE WAS CONDEMNED"

While JESUS is being dragged through the city, over which He had wept, to Pilate's Hall, we must fix our attention on another of the Apostles—"he that was called Judas"—and see what he is doing. We find him engaged in a deed so dark, that only one of the Evangelists, St. Matthew, can find the courage to say anything about it. Peter is obliged to refer to it, to the little company of "brethren" during the Novena before the first Whit-Sunday, for it was his duty to see that someone was appointed to fill "the place from which Judas had by transgression fallen." (Acts i. 25.)

"*Seeing* that He was condemned." It may be that Judas had lingered near enough to know that his Master had been found guilty of death before the Jewish tribunals, and that He was on His way to have the sentence of death passed at the Roman tribunal. Or it may be, as a striking picture suggests, that the truth was rudely brought home to him by his coming unexpectedly, in the early dawn, upon *the cross* lying on the ground; the two workmen who had hastily cut down the wood and put it together, worn out with their night's work, are sleeping by it. Judas is staggered—aghast! He *sees* that he has gone too far. Jesus is *not* going to save Himself. He is condemned, and he, Judas Iscariot, is the cause of His death. Judas is alone with his sin, and a blank despair seizes him.

POINT II.

REPENTING HIMSELF, HE SAID: I HAVE SINNED

The realisation of the lengths to which he has allowed Satan to lead him is too much; he repents, makes restitution, confesses his sin, and declares his Master innocent. "What more is wanting? Does it not almost look as if he had the three things which the Catechism says are necessary on the part of the penitent—contrition, confession, and satisfaction? *Almost,* but not quite. The important thing was not there. Judas had no *contrition*—not one spark, or "his own place" would never have been hell, (Acts i. 25), and JESUS

107

would never have said of him: It were better for him if that man had not been born. (St Mark xiv. 21.) Repentance, a change of mind, he had; for, till the moment when he saw that JESUS was condemned, he had thought that He would save Himself; now his point of view was completely changed. But there was not in that dark heart one thought of GOD, nor of how he had grieved Him, not one thought of his own sinfulness and ingratitude. He made his confession and satisfaction to the wrong people, whose only answer could be: "What is that to us?" His state was one of abject despair, without any beautiful contrition to soften it. His repentance was remorse—the remorse of those in hell—Satan's reward to his wretched victims.

POINT III.

"HE WENT AND HANGED HIMSELF"

And so he hurried himself into eternity. And the next moment he was alone with his sin in the presence of Him Whom he dared not face on earth—in the presence of that GOD Whom he had betrayed, and Who was no longer his loving, sorrowing Friend, but his inexorable Judge.

Satan had finished his ghastly work, without let or hindrance.

And yet, St Peter says: "He was numbered with us, and obtained part of the ministry." (Acts i. 17.) He had had just the same advantages and privileges, a part of the ministry had been entrusted to him; but little by little he had separated himself, little by little he had allowed the love of gain to exclude the love of GOD, little by little Satan had taken possession of his heart, and his only ambition had been to get rich at whatever cost. And now suddenly all has failed; he has nothing left; he cares no longer for the thirty pieces of silver, which a few hours before he had deemed such a prize—that "handsome price that I was prized by them!" (Zech. xi. 13.) There is nothing left to live for, and he is too blinded to fear death.

It was too late for Judas to save JESUS, but it was not too late for him to save his own soul. One look towards JESUS, one spark of sorrow, one desire for pardon would have been enough. But in his hardened heart none of these could be found; he had deliberately steeled himself against all good influences, till he desired nothing but sin; his hell had already begun, and "he departed, and went and hanged himself with an halter."

So the Church brings me to the very brink of hell, and bids me look well at it this Lent, remembering that if it was a possibility for one of the chosen twelve, it is a possibility for me. It is not for nothing that every Priest, just before the solemn moment of Consecration, prays: "*ab æterna damnatione nos eripi*" (that we be snatched from eternal damnation); and just before giving himself Holy Communion, when he is face to face with his GOD, what is his prayer? "*A Te nunquam separari permittas*" (Never suffer me to be separated from Thee). Never suffer me to go to hell. Hell is the direct consequence of sin, and I have sinned. I deserve to be there, and it is only because of GOD's mercy that I am not. Let me think over these facts, and take in all humility the warning given me by my loving Master: "Fear Him who hath power to cast into hell; yea, I say to you, fear Him." (St Luke xii. 5.)

Colloquy with JESUS, for I dare not talk about hell to anyone else.

Resolution, Never to turn a deaf ear to Conscience about the smallest thing.

Spiritual Bouquet. "Thou art just, O Lord: and Thy judgment is right." (Ps. cxviii. 137.)

— ❧ —

Jesus before Pilate

Fourth Week. Wednesday.

"Christ Jesus Who gave testimony under Pontius Pilate, a good confession." (1 Tim. vi. 13.)

> 1st *Prelude.* Jesus standing with His accusers, outside the Prætorium.
> 2nd *Prelude.* The grace to keep near, and learn the lessons.

Point I.
Outside the Prætorium

It was very early in the morning when Jesus got to the end of His painful walk across Jerusalem, and He is standing now outside the Prætorium waiting for the Roman Governor to confirm the sentence of death. Pilate is a pagan, and his dealings with Jesus will not have the power to wound His Heart, as do those of His own nation. It is in proportion to my knowledge and love of Jesus that my sins and infidelities cause Him pain.

The Jews cannot cross a heathen threshold, for they must not be defiled during the Festival time, (St John xviii. 28), so Pilate comes out to them. Directly he sees that the Prisoner is in chains, he knows that the Jews wish for a capital sentence, but he is not going to pass it without hearing the accusations. "What accusations bring you against this Man?" he asks. They are annoyed, thinking that it ought to be sufficient for Pilate that their Courts consider Him guilty of death; and they answer testily: "If He were not a malefactor, we would not have delivered Him up to thee." "Take Him," retorts Pilate, "and judge Him according to your law." Their answer shows plainly what they want: "It is not lawful for *us* to put any man to *death.*" And JESUS is standing by listening! But what are the accusations? persists Pilate. They choose the three which they think would be the most likely to carry weight with the Governor: He perverts our nation, He forbids to give tribute to Cæsar, and He says that He is Christ, a King. The absolute absurdity of this last charge is too much for Pilate. His accusers have gone too far and harmed their own cause. Pilate's sympathies are aroused in favour of the Prisoner, he will take Him away and examine Him alone. It may be that he had heard something about JESUS from his wife, who had perhaps already begun to take an interest in the GOD of the Jews, and in the Prophet Who talked so much about Him. So he called JESUS into the Hall.

POINT II.

INSIDE THE PRÆTORIUM

Now they are alone—the Roman Governor and the abject-looking Prisoner in chains. Pilate looks at Him: "*Thou*—art *Thou* a King! and the King of the Jews?" The supreme thought in the mind of JESUS is Pilate's salvation. He reads his inmost thoughts, and tries to make him true to himself. Nothing had been said to Pilate about His being King of *the Jews,* and so JESUS asks quietly: "Sayest thou this thing of thyself, or have others (perhaps his wife) told it thee of Me?" Pilate answers hotly: "Am I a Jew?" What dealings have I with them? It is they, your own people, who have delivered you up to me. What have you done? That is what I, as your judge, must know. JESUS, however, takes no notice of the question. He knows that Pilate's conscience is uneasy, and that he is wondering still whether He *can* be a King, and, if so, where His Kingdom is; and so He tells him plainly: "*My Kingdom is not of this world*"; if it were, My subjects would fight for Me, and not allow Me to be delivered up to the Jews. Then He has got a Kingdom somewhere, thinks Pilate, and he asks: "Thou *art* a King then?" And JESUS answers emphatically: "Thou sayest that I am a King." What thou sayest is indeed true, I will not hide it from thee, for my reason for being in the world at all, is to bear witness to the truth; *and* He adds, hoping to touch Pilate: "Everyone that is of the truth, heareth My Voice." Will Pilate hear His Voice? Will he listen to his conscience, which is now speaking so plainly? No, he feels that if he is to do his work he must cut short this interview; the Prisoner is exerting an influence over him for which he cannot account, and which he does not want, so saying brusquely: "What is truth?" he goes back again with JESUS to the Jews.

What a chance Pilate lost! It was his moment of grace, and he let it pass. He was face to face with the Truth itself, Who would have answered his question, but he neither waited nor cared.

Let us be careful about our moments of grace—they soon pass—and let us pray for the many souls who during this Lent are having opportunities offered to them, that they may not waste them, as Pilate did.

POINT III

"I FIND NO CAUSE"

The Jews are waiting eagerly for the verdict, and they watch the two coming back together. "*I find no cause in the Man,*" Pilate declares; he is bold and fearless for once and says what he thinks—the result perhaps of his being in such close contact with the Truth. Then "the Chief Priests accused Him in many things," (St Mark xv. 3), and, to their accusations, JESUS answered nothing. Pilate "wondered exceedingly" at His silence, he could not understand it. "Answerest Thou nothing; behold how great testimonies they allege against Thee." (St Matt. xxvii. 13.) But "He answered him to never a word."

Would I really be like Him this Lent? One very simple way—though no one, before trying it, would guess how hard it is—would be, to say nothing when I am falsely accused; not if something is in question about which the truth ought to be known, but when it is some little trifling thing, my silence about which will inconvenience nobody but myself.

His accusers are getting anxious, and they say more earnestly: "He stirreth up the people, teaching throughout all Judæa, beginning from Galilee." (St Luke xxiii. 5.) Pilate catches the word *Galilee,* and sees in it a way out of his difficulties. Is the Prisoner a Man of Galilee? he asks. Ah, then as a simple matter of courtesy I must send Him to Herod, for He is under his jurisdiction.

"The Kings of the earth stood up, and the princes met together, against the Lord, and against His Christ. He that dwelleth in Heaven shall laugh at them. ... I am appointed King by Him over Sion." (Ps. ii. 2-6.)

If He is *my* King, I need fear nothing—not even being called upon to share His humiliations.

Colloquy with my King in chains.

Resolution. To accompany Him in His journeyings to and fro, by thinking constantly of Him.

Spiritual Bouquet. "I am appointed King."

Again before Pilate

"And Herod sent Him back to Pilate" (St Luke sxiii. 11.)

1ˢᵗ Prelude.   Jesus in the fool's garment.
2ⁿᵈ Prelude.   Grace to stand by, and learn the lessons He intend for *me*.

Point I.
Herod and Pilate become friends

Herod could get absolutely nothing out of Jesus, and pretending on that account that he believed Him to be a madman, he dressed Him in a fool's garment, and after he and his courtiers "had set Him at nought and mocked Him," (St Luke xxiii. 11), he sent Him back to Pilate, By this interchange of courtesies, at the expense of Jesus, the Roman Governor and King Herod were reconciled after their quarrel. "They were made friends that same day." Both acknowledged that the Prisoner was innocent, yet they leagued themselves together against Him. It is only the *world's* peace that they have got. Jesus does not give them *His* peace; He reserves that for His friends.

Which peace do I really value most? the peace that Jesus gives to those who love Him and put Him first at whatever cost? or the peace that comes from compromise with the world and following its maxims?

Point II.
"I will therefore chastise him"

Pilate now makes another attempt to save the Prisoner. With Jesus standing at his side in the fool's garment, he addresses the chief priests and the people: You have brought all sorts of charges against this Man, but neither I, nor Herod, can find any reason in them for the capital punishment. He must be made to understand, however, that He must not "pervert the people" any more. I will therefore *chastise* Him and release Him. The word used for *chastise is* a mild one—the same as that used in Hebrews xii. 6: "Whom the Lord loveth, He *chastiseth*." It means to correct as one corrects a child, to make him understand that he must not transgress again.

So Pilate tries to compromise. He knows that JESUS is innocent, yet he dare not offend the Jews by failing to punish a prisoner accused of perverting the people, for Cæsar would be sure to hear of it, and then it is Pilate who will suffer.

I have not far to go to find a parallel. Am I always strong for the right whatever it costs? Do I know nothing of compromise—giving way just a little for the sake of what people will think or say? Do I never turn a deaf ear to conscience, and even do something that I know will not quite bear the light, rather than displease someone whose good opinion I want to keep? It was through weakness that Pilate made the mistake of his life; let me be warned, and set my face against all vacillating and hesitating, where truth is concerned.

POINT III.

PILATE'S WIFE

Yet another expedient presents itself to Pilate's mind. It is the Parasceve, the day on which pardon is always granted to some prisoner. The choice rests with the Jewish people. Perhaps, thinks Pilate, they will choose JESUS, if it is suggested to them; so he brings out a notorious prisoner, and putting him alongside of JESUS, he asks: "Whom will you,

Barabbas or Jesus?" And "the whole multitude together cries out: Away with this Man, and release unto us Barabbas."

Just at this critical moment Pilate received a message from his wife. She knew, probably, that her husband was in favour of the Prisoner; but she knew also the weakness of his character, and hearing the shouts of the mob, and knowing full well what they meant, she was terribly afraid that he would be swayed by them. Her message was:

"Have thou nothing to do with that Just Man, for I have suffered many things this day in a dream because of Him." She was a pagan like her husband, yet she was the only one who found courage to plead the cause of Jesus. She was rewarded by the gift of the faith, and the Feast of Claudia Procula is kept in the Eastern Church on October 27th.

Thus does GOD give Pilate one more chance, one more warning; but it is useless, he will not listen. The people, "persuaded by the chief priests," are still clamouring for Barabbas. "What shall I do, then, with Jesus?" Pilate asks weakly. "Crucify Him, crucify Him!" is the unanimous cry. "But why, what evil hath He done? I find no cause of death in Him"; and again he suggests chastisement and release. This is the third time that Pilate has proclaimed His innocence. But the people will have none of it, and Pilate sees that it is they who are going to prevail.

POINT IV.

PILATE WASHES HIS HANDS

Pilate orders water to be brought, and he washes his hands before them. All understand the significance of this act—it means that the Governor will hold out no longer; it means that he considers the prisoner innocent; and it means that he does not consider himself to be in any way responsible for

His death. "I am innocent of the blood of this Just Man. (The fourth time!) Look ye to it." And, delighted at having gained the day, they cry out: "His Blood be upon us and upon our children." Thus the Jews take the blame on themselves for ever. And Pilate, can he thus wash his hands of all responsibility? Ah, no, God will hold him guilty for acting against his conscience, and for taking no notice of the warnings He gave him.

It is not an unknown thing for me to act very much as Pilate did—shifting the blame on to others, and trying to square my conscience by pretending that I have no responsibility in the matter. However well I may wash my hands, I am not innocent of His Blood any more than Pilate was. And I hurt Him far more than Pilate did. Let me go and stand by Him as He waits there patiently in the fool's garment; let me throw in my lot with Him openly and whole-heartedly; let me tell Him that I am determined that there shall be no more hesitation and weakness, no more wavering, and pretending that I am not responsible. So shall I give Him consolation.

Colloquy with Jesus, telling Him how sorry I am for the many occasions in which I, too, have resisted the grace offered to me, and begging Him to let me once again wash my soiled hands in His Blood.

Resolution. To spend today standing by Jesus in the fool's garment.

Spiritual Bouquet. "His Blood be upon us."

Ecce Homo!

Fourth Week. Friday.

"JESUS therefore came forth, bearing the crown of thorns and the purple garment." (St John xix. 5.)

1st *Prelude.*   Picture of the "Ecce Homo."
2nd *Prelude.*   Grace and courage to behold the Man.

From the Campion Missal and Hymnal

POINT I.
"JESUS HE DELIVERED UP TO THEIR WILL"

Pilate, after washing his hands and pretending to himself that his conscience was clear, released Barabbas, "and having *scourged* JESUS, delivered Him unto them to be crucified." The word used for the scourging is no longer the mild one, but the one that signifies that terrible Roman punishment which few of its victims survived. "According to the measure of the sin shall the measure also of the stripes be." (Deut. xxv. 2.) What was the measure of the sin in this case? "The Lord hath laid on Him the iniquity of us *all*." (Isaias liii. 6.) "For the wickedness of My people have I struck Him." (verse 8.)

"JESUS he delivered up to their will," (St Luke xxiii, 25), that is, to the will of the brutal Roman soldiers, and, their will was to *mock* Him because He called Himself a King. There were no restrictions to their brutality, for the Prisoner was condemned to death. They took Him back into the Hall, put a scarlet cloak round Him, a crown of thorns on His Head, and a reed in His Hands for a sceptre; then "bowing the knee before Him, they mocked Him, saying: Hail, King of the Jews. And spitting upon Him, they took the reed and struck His Head!" The "whole band," that is, a cohort (600 men), took part in this disgraceful scene. The Centurion must have been with them. Did he too take part? or was the marvellous patience of JESUS already beginning to do its blessed work in another heathen soul?

Pilate now comes out again, and, seeing the pitiable state to which the Prisoner is reduced, his compassion is once more stirred, and he hopes that, at the sight of Him, the people may be touched too, and the sentence after all reversed.

POINT II.

ECCE HOMO!

He brings Him forth, puts Him where all can see Him; and cries: "*Behold the Man!*" But no spark of pity is to be found in their hardened hearts—the scarlet cloak, the crown of thorns, the reed, His bleeding wounds, His faltering steps—all these are nothing to them.

What are they to me? Let me stay and look at Him; for in that Man I see my King, my GOD, and my Savior; and I must offer Him—for He needs all He can get from His friends now—my faith, my adoration, and my love.

(1) He is my *King*. I have sworn to serve Him. His Kingdom alone shall stand, and He shall reign for ever and ever. Once more on my knees I make an *Act of Faith* in my King, and in His Kingdom; once more do I thank Him with all my heart for making me a member of that Kingdom; once again do I promise Him to be a loyal subject—that is, a subject who understands that my King has the right to command me without consulting me, or giving any reasons for His dealings with me.

(2) He is my *God*. The Roman soldiers bent the knee in mockery, but I will make a humble *Act of Adoration* before the little Host under whose form my GOD is as surely hidden as He was under the bleeding form of the Prisoner standing at the Tribunal. And as I say: "My GOD, I adore Thee," I will tell Him that I want to make some little reparation for the mockery of Pilate's soldiers.

(3) Behold the *Man!* He is my *Savior*. All this terrible suffering that He is undergoing is for me. He is atoning for my sins. He is getting merit for me. He is making it possible for me to save my soul, by paying every particle of the penalty that is due to GOD's justice. Oh, what an infinite love is the

love of my King! Let me try to repay it by my *Acts of Love.* Let me never tire of telling Him that I love Him, trying to believe that He never tires of hearing me. Let me tell Him that the result of watching so carefully all the details of His Passion is an increase of love; that I am more than ever determined that "in what place soever my Lord the King is, there will I, His servant, be," (2 Kings xv. 21), be it in false accusation, misunderstanding, suffering—even mockery and degradation and cruelty. Whatever place it *is,* my King is there, and therefore it is my place too. Only love can attain to this, and nothing short of this, can satisfy love. Once again, then, I will behold the Man, and will say with all my heart, a heart that is breaking at the thought of His sufferings: My King, my God, my Savior, I love Thee.

Point III.

the son of God

"When they had seen Him they cried out again: Crucify Him, crucify Him!" Such inhuman want of pity is revolting even to the heathen Governor, and he answers in irony, for he knows his proposition is an impossible one: "Take Him *you* and crucify Him, for I find no cause in Him." (The fifth time!) Then the Jews, who are now getting anxious in case, after all, the vacillating Pilate should refuse to condemn Him to death; speak the *truth,* and bring forward the only real charge which they have against Him, the Prisoner. They had kept it in the background because they did not think it likely to appeal to Pilate: "We have a law, and according to the law. He ought to die, because He *made Himself the Son of God."* The real cause for their hatred of Jesus is out now. They play their last card, and they hope that Pilate will see things, from their point of view. Their High Priest had said that the sin was one of blasphemy, and that was a sin punishable with death. (Levit. xxiv. 16.) The Prisoner, then, *must* be put to death; *they* cannot do it, Pilate *can,* and the Roman punishment for a capital offence is crucifixion. It is all so logical!

And JESUS is still standing waiting. Under the scarlet cloak His Sacred Heart is beating with love for His people, and beating with joy because every moment is bringing the cross nearer.

> *Colloquy* with my King, offering Him again my faith, my adoration, and my love.
>
> *Resolution.* To remember, in any trial that may be in store for me today, that I have promised to be where my King is.
>
> *Spiritual Bouquet.* "Ecce Homo!"

Still before Pilate

Fourth Week. Saturday.

"When, He was reviled, He did not revile: when He suffered. He threatened not, but delivered Himself to him that judged Him unjustly." (1 Pet. ii. 23.)

> *1st Prelude.* JESUS still dressed as a King.
> *2nd Prelude.* The grace never to deliver Him up.

POINT I.
"WHENCE ART THOU?"

"When Pilate heard this, he feared the more." The logic of the Jews is not appealing to him just now. He has heard one thing, and one thing only—"*the Son of GOD.*" What if it should be true! It might be—and if so, it would throw light on his wife's dream, and would account for the wonderful patience of Jesus. Once more He takes Him aside, away from the people. Once more they are alone—Christ, the only begotten Son of GOD, and Pontius Pilate, under whom He suffered. "Whence art Thou?" Pilate asks, meaning: Are you really the Son of GOD? JESUS gives him no answer. Pilate is astonished at His calm, quiet dignity, and at His courage. "Speakest Thou not to me? Knowest Thou not that I have power to crucify Thee, and I have power to release Thee?" Then JESUS speaks of His Father, and tells Pilate that, however powerful he may think himself to be, he has only just as much power as GOD gives him, and will only do just what GOD wills to be done. And, He adds: He that delivered Me to you, that is, the Jewish nation, hath a greater sin than yours; your sin is one of weakness, theirs is one of hatred.

POINT II.
WHO DELIVERED JESUS TO DEATH?

(1) *Pilate.* "He *delivered* Him to them to be crucified," (St John xix. 16.) The Church never lets us forget it. He "suffered under Pontius Pilate." But Pilate was less guilty than the Jews. There are many excuses to be made for him. His sin was that he condemned, against his conscience, an innocent man—he was a homicide but not deicide. Whenever we think of him, let us ask for grace never in the smallest thing to act against conscience. And we may always hope that the legend is true, which makes Pilate, in his remorse, seek and find grace.

(2) *Judas.* "What will you give me, and I will *deliver* Him unto you?" (St Matt. xxvi. l5.)

(3) *The Jews.* "Thy own nation and the Chief Priests have *delivered* Thee up." (St John xviii. 35.) All those, whose was "the greater sin"—Annas and Caiaphas, (for envy); the

scribes, (in spite of their knowledge of Prophecies); His own people, who had seen His miracles and heard His teaching?

(4) *All sinners.* I, every time that I sin wilfully, *deliver* Him up, "Who loved me and delivered Himself for me." (Gal.ii.20.)

(5) *JESUS,* "Who *delivered* Himself to him that judged Him unjustly." (1 Pet. ii. 23.) "Christ also hath loved us, and hath *delivered* Himself for us." (Eph. v. 2.)

(6) GOD *the Father,* Who "spared not even His Own Son, but *delivered* Him up for us all." (Rom. viii. 32.)

O my JESUS, once more I look at Thee standing there with Pilate. One thought is absorbing Thee—my soul and my salvation. Thou art delivering Thyself for me, that I, who have "the greater sin," may go free. What amazing love!

How can I show my gratitude? By promising Him now, at once, while He is standing in the scarlet cloak and wearing the crown of thorns, that I will never again wilfully deliver Him up. *Self* shall be delivered up, but never JESUS.

POINT III.
"PILATE GAVE SENTENCE" (ST LUKE XXIII. 24)

Pilate, touched probably by the lenient way in which JESUS had judged his conduct, goes back to the Jews, determined to use every effort to release Him. "But the Jews cry out, saying: If thou release this Man, thou art not Cæsar's friend; for whoever maketh himself a king, speaketh against Cæsar." They revert again to the political charge, and intend Pilate to understand that Cæsar shall hear of it if he fails to condemn a prisoner accused of sedition. Pilate does understand, and he knows that such a charge would mean that he himself would be condemned for treason. He must choose, then, between himself and JESUS. His choice is quickly made; he sits down in the judgment-seat, and has JESUS brought forth. "It was the sixth hour" of the Parasceve. John notices the time of this most momentous moment. As Pilate sees Him coming, still dressed as a King, he says to the people: "Behold your King!" But they cry out: "Away with Him: Away with Him: Crucify Him!" Pilate saith to them: "Shall I crucify your King?" The Chief Priests answer: "We have no king but Cæsar." Pilate can hold out no longer. He "gave sentence that it should be as they required." He delivered Him to them to be crucified. "And they took Jesus, and led Him forth."

Thus Pilate saves himself at the expense of Jesus. It is impossible for him to save both. And it is impossible for me too. Which am I making up my mind to save this Lent, Jesus or self? Am I steadily, and perseveringly, and without any quarter, putting to death the "old man," self, "with all its affections and lusts;" or am I allowing him to live and flourish at the expense of Jesus, whom I crucify afresh every time that I sin? (Heb. vi. 6.)

> *Colloquy* with Jesus led forth to be crucified for me.
>
> *Resolution.* Never to deliver Him up—not even by a wilful imperfection.
>
> *Spiritual Bouquet.* "He that delivered Me . . . hath the greater sin."

The Way of the Cross (I)

Passion Sunday.

"They took off the cloak from Him, and put on Him His own garments, and led Him away to crucify Him." (St Matt. xxvii. 31.)

1ˢᵗ Prelude.   Jesus on the Prætorium steps, for the sixth time. He wears His own robe, His Feet are bare, His Head crowned.

2ⁿᵈ Prelude.   The grace to follow in His steps.

POINT I.
THE CROSS

He is in their power at last! With what fierce delight do they tear off the scarlet cloak, regardless of the pain they are causing His bruised and bleeding Body. They put on His Own garment—the precious seamless robe—but they leave the crown of thorns on His Head to torture Him to the end. He descends the steps to the howling mob below, where His executioners are waiting for Him with the Cross. What calm dignity! What perfect submission! What courage possessed Him as He went to receive His Cross! And something else too, and that was *joy*—joy because His Hour was come. The Cross had been the dream of His life, and now nothing stood between Him and it. "Greater love hath no man than this!" (St John xv. 13.)

From whom did JESUS receive His Cross? From the rough, brutal executioners, who were gloating over their Victim? From the Jews, who had said: "We have a law, and by our law He ought to die"? (St John xix. 7.) From the Chief Priests and the Council, who had "sought for evidence and found none"? (St Mark xiv. 55.) From the Scribes and Pharisees, who were rejoicing in the thought that they had won the day? From Pilate, who had proudly said: "I have power to crucify Thee"? (St John xix. 10.) From His Own people, who had shouted with one accord: "Let Him be crucified. His Blood be upon us"? (St Matt. xxvii. 23, 25.) Yes, from all these, and yet from none of them, for He looked beyond them all to His Father; straight from His Hands He took His Cross, saying: "The chalice which My Father hath given Me, shall I not drink it?" (St John xviii. 11.) "Behold I come to do Thy Will, O My GOD. I have desired it." (Ps. xxxix. 8.)

How much trouble and anguish I should save myself if only I could learn the lesson that Jesus is teaching me! He is showing me how to receive my crosses, bidding me look away from second causes to God, Who is the first cause of all that can possibly happen to me. Much of my difficulty, in carrying my little daily crosses, is caused by my not having learned this lesson. I am so taken up with the different people whom God employs to hand me the cross, that I very often lose sight altogether of the fact that it comes directly from Him, and in the exact form too in which I receive it. It may be perfectly true that this one hands it to me from want of charity, another from sinister motives, a third from tactlessness, another from a love of interference, another from a deliberate wish to harm me—but these are only *the second causes,* and they are not so bad as those Jesus had to bear! Do not let me waste time, and precious opportunities of grace, by fixing my mind on these, and brooding over them, and allowing them to make me sad, and sore, and even angry; but let me rather, as my Master did, look beyond them all to my Father, fix my eyes so intently on Him that I cannot see the second causes, take the little crosses straight from His Hands, and thank Him for giving me one more mark of His special favour.

Point II.

Jesus falls beneath the cross

"And bearing His Own Cross, He went forth to that place which is called Calvary." (St John xix. 17.) No murmur nor complaint escapes Him as the executioners lay the heavy cross on His bruised and aching shoulders, Tired and exhausted and suffering though He is, He sets Himself to His impossible task. He has not gone far before He staggers and falls.

His wounds re-open, and His Blood flows anew. Why does He allow Himself to fall? Because, in the excess of His love, He would atone for my falls, and gain merit for me when I get up again and go on perseveringly as He did. If I am climbing the hill of perfection, I shall fall—probably often. It is better to fall over climbing it, than never to fall because I never attempt to climb. But what use do I make of my falls? Are they a means of perfection? or are they a hindrance on the road?

As I look again at JESUS on His knees I notice how sad He looks. What is the cause of His sadness? His sufferings, the jeers of the crowd, the cruel blows of the soldiers—yes, all these, but may not He also have been sad because His journey towards Calvary was being hindered, the moment of His Sacrifice that He was longing to accomplish delayed? He is sad, but He is calm and resigned, there is no impatience with His executioners, nor with circumstances, nor with Himself. Neither is He astonished at His fall, for He knows how weak He is. Let me learn from my Master, Who fell for my sake. I fall, and I am sad—and rightly. But what is the cause of my sadness? Is it because I am hindered on my road to perfection? Is it because the fulfilment of my end seems a little further off than I had hoped? Is it because my fall has grieved the loving Heart of JESUS? Or does my sadness come from wounded pride, from annoyance that I have failed again, from impatience with myself and everybody else, because I am not what I thought I was?

O my JESUS, as I watch Thee struggling to get up and go on again, Thy determination to reach the top of the hill intensified by Thy fall, I will tell Thee something which will console Thee for this hindrance, which Thou didst permit for me. That from henceforth I am determined when I fall:

1. To lose no time grovelling on the ground (occasions of sin).

2. To get up at once, (contrition), anxious to make up for delay, (reparation).

3. Not to be so terribly surprised at my falls, (humility).

4. To go on again more carefully, more humbly, more trustfully, more joyfully, my desire for perfection and for the Cross intensified by my fall, (perseverance).

Colloquy with Jesus, Who received His Cross, carried it, and fell under its weight for me.

Resolution. To receive mine, and carry it for Him and to let even my falls redound to His glory.

Spiritual Bouquet. "Even the death of the Cross (Phil. ii. 8.)

The Way of the Cross (2)

Passion Week. Monday.

"O all ye that pass by the way, attend." (Lam. i. 12.)

1ˢᵗ Prelude.   Jesus carrying His Cross.
2ⁿᵈ Prelude.   The grace and courage to go to meet Him.

Point I.
His Mother

"*Fourth Station. Jesus meets His Blessed Mother!* Familiar words; let me try, today, to understand more fully what they mean. The meeting took place just after His fall. She probably saw the fall, and possibly occasioned it. It may have been that it was the sight of His Mother, with the knowledge of the agony she was suffering, which made His Cross more than He could bear.

Mary knows *all* that has happened since the agony in the Garden last night, for, though hidden, she has never been far away. Now, in spite of all the pain which she knows it will cost both herself and her Son, she goes to meet the Procession. It is coming now. What a sight for a Mother! Her Son, Whom she had seen only such a short while ago in all the beauty and strength of His Manhood, now walking as a criminal through the city, weak and suffering, staggering under the weight of His Cross. The heavy end is on His shoulder, the other dragging on the ground and jolting His emaciated, wounded Body at every step. He sees His Mother; for a moment their eyes meet—it is enough, each knows the other's pain. No word is spoken; there is no need, they understand each other perfectly. Those two hearts loved each other more than any other hearts have ever loved, and yet neither would raise a finger to spare the other suffering—both understood its value too well.

When I have to witness pain and suffering, for which it is impossible to see the reason; or when I have to bear the unutterable pain of having to inflict suffering on those who cannot, and who never will in this world, understand why I do it, let me remember that it was because Jesus loved Mary more than anyone else that He gave her a larger share of suffering than He gave to anyone else.

But there is joy as well as pain in that meeting. Mary is still saying her *Magnificat* as well as her *Fiat*. She has long been in the secret. She saw this picture in which she is now taking a part before she consented to become His Mother. She knew all that it involved when she said at the Incarnation: "Be it unto me according to Thy word." Now, she alone of all the spectators understands. She sees written large over the terrible picture: "*He shall save His people from their sins.*" He is the Redeemer of the world; and, because all her Son's interests are hers, because she understands that He is going to His shameful death to fulfil His Father's Will and the desire of His Own Heart, because she knows that all is happening with His full permission, and that His Heart is full of joy, her sorrowing heart is full of joy too.

Such is the result of a perfect union with JESUS—joy and peace in the midst of sorrow and suffering. What do I know about it?

POINT II.

SIMON THE CYRENEAN

"I looked for one that would comfort me, and I found none." (Ps. lxviii. 21.) He needed help. It was impossible for Him to go on—even His enemies saw that. He found none. None would disgrace himself by touching the cross of a criminal. JESUS does not expect help from the soldiers nor from the hooting crowd, but where are His friends? Are there none in that crowd who have listened to His teaching, whom He has comforted, healed, restored to life? none who are grateful, none who love Him? If so, their love and gratitude does not go far enough; they dare not identify themselves with Him to the point of bearing His Cross. *I found none.*

JESUS is still looking through the eyes of His poor, His little ones, His sick, His afflicted, lonely, tempted, weary ones. Does He always get for them just the help that He is looking for, from me? Or does He have to say sadly: "I looked for . . . comfort . . . and I found none"? That *does* love Me, but not enough—not to the point of self-denial.

The Chief Priests have found someone—Simon, a countryman coming home from his work; they are bargaining with him, and *compelling* him, for the case is urgent. Very unwillingly Simon takes the Criminal's place, but tradition tells us that no sooner had he begun his distasteful work than he became another man. Was it the sight of that Figure in front of him, pitiful, worn out, yet patient and uncomplaining, that wrought the sudden change in his heart, or was it the touch of the Cross of JESUS? We know not, but we know that he stopped his complaining, and became a true disciple, that is, one who carries his cross after JESUS. The Cross is already beginning to do its work, and JESUS and Mary have another joy to help them along the Way of Sorrows. Do I give them this joy and consolation, that of seeing me bearing my cross after JESUS, and thus making His lighter?

POINT III.

VERONICA

JESUS has another soul to convert as He passes along the Way of Sorrows. A noble Roman lady is struck with the look of innocence and patience on the Face of the Criminal. His face is covered not only with blood from the thorn-wounds and dust from the road, but, shameful to say, with spittle too; and, with a woman's instinct, Veronica notices that, His hands being occupied with the Cross, He cannot even give Himself the relief of wiping His Face. Did He give her one of His looks? We do not know, but we do know that in an instant she was at His side, wiping His Face with her own veil, which, regardless of the etiquette due to her rank, she had torn off. His look of loving gratitude touched her pagan heart, and yet another disciple was ready to take up her cross and carry it after JESUS. The wonderful picture of that suffering Face, which Veronica found traced upon her veil,[1] was indeed a precious memento, but the picture which Veronica will never forget is the one impressed on her heart.

---

[1] St Veronica's veil is amongst the treasures of the Vatican Basilica. It is exposed for the veneration of the faithful every Holy Week.

JESUS is just as grateful now as He was then for all the little acts of charity that are done to Him in the person of His brethren. Each act puts another touch to the Image of Himself which He is tracing in our hearts. Each act makes the likeness a little more like. If I realised this, should I not be a *little* more charitable than I am? The Divine Image can only be impressed in my heart by the effacement of the image of self—that is, by self-denial and mortification. The only likeness of her Son that Mary will recognize is one traced in tears and blood.

> *Colloquy* with JESUS carrying His Cross for me.
>
> *Resolution.* To go out today to meet Him, and to give Him whatever help He needs.
>
> *Spiritual Bouquet.* "As long as you did it to one of these My least brethren, you did it to Me." (St Matt. xxv. 40.)

The Hill of Calvary

Passion Week. Tuesday.

"And they came to the place that is called Golgotha, which is the place of Calvary." (St Matt. xxvii. *33.*)

1ˢᵗ Prelude. The Hill of Calvary.
2ⁿᵈ Prelude. The grace to keep very close to JESUS.

POINT I.
THE DAUGHTERS OF JERUSALEM

Just at the foot of Calvary the Procession is again at a standstill. Some more women are offering their sympathy, and He must show His gratitude to them too. These are not pagans;

they have had many opportunities of knowing Him; He it is Who blessed their babes, healed their sick, taught in their streets, and was ever ready to show sympathy to all. JESUS must say one word to them—it is His only recorded word on the Way of Sorrows, and it is a word of warning. He has not to say to *them;* "O all ye that pass by, attend." They have *not* passed by, they *are* attending. What, then, is wanting? He is afraid of their sorrow being a too *natural* one, and not going to the root of the matter. Weep not for Me, weep for yourselves and for your children, and for all the evil that is coming on your nation; if the green tree (a just Man) is treated; like this, what will happen to the dry wood *(sinners)?.* Weep for the *cause* of My suffering—for sin—for your own sins.

What is the lesson, then, that He stops to give to these daughters of Jerusalem, and through them to us all? That He values our sympathy in proportion to the amount of contrition that prompts it. Let me try to put the lesson into practice this Passion-tide.

POINT II.

JESUS IS STRIPPED OF HIS GARMENTS

The top of Calvary's hill was reached at last, and the soldiers, as was the custom, offered JESUS a cup of wine and gall to deaden His sufferings. *"But He took it not."* He preferred His Father's cup to any mixed by human hands. Quickly the executioners set about their business. First His clothes, which have been pressed by the weight of the Cross into the wounds, are torn off, and the Precious Blood flows again. There is no consideration, no gentleness, no alleviation for *Him.* It is Himself Who is arranging every detail of His Passion, and they are being arranged not to spare Himself, but out of an *excess* of love for us, to merit, to expiate, and to set us an example.

It is difficult to stand by and see Him treated with such unnecessary cruelty, and I begin to feel rather like Peter did, when he drew his sword in the Garden; but the Master calms me, as He did him, by explaining, and making the matter a personal one: You will not be too particular after this, about getting every possible alleviation for your pain and suffering, will you? Alleviate that of others, and in so doing you will alleviate Mine. But for yourself, unite your suffering to Mine, look upon it as a precious gift from Me, use it for My Father's glory, for the expiation of sin, for your own sanctification, and for all the Intentions of My Sacred Heart. Do not let one drop of the precious cup be wasted, and remember that those who suffer for Me are doing a great work.

But Jesus is suffering something worse than pain. He the All-holy, the All-pure is stripped before His creatures. Mary turns away her face from a sight so distressing, but can I, *dare* I, turn away mine when I know for what He is atoning? As I think of Him exposed to the rude, coarse, curious gaze of all who would, let me learn, by the price He paid to merit it for me, the value He sets on holy Purity, and let me make an Act of Contrition. He allows Himself to be stripped of His garments—His last possession. He has given up everything else before, and has lived a life of poverty, deprivation, and hardship, in order to teach me to love and practice detachment for His sake. Again He seems to be speaking to my heart: Is there anything, My child, to which you are still attached? anything which you would not be ready to give up, the moment I asked for it? anything which is, little by little, winding itself round your heart—that heart which has been given to *Me,* and of which I am jealous?

Point III
The First Word

He has stretched Himself on the Cross now, for He is *obedient* to His executioners as His Father's instruments—*even unto death*. As they knock in the nails He utters His first word from the Cross: "*Father, forgive them, for they know not what they do*." He mentions none by name, He excludes none—all sinners, past, present, future. They none of them know really, or they could not sin against such love, "Father," the Father of all the children for whom I am being crucified, "forgive them"; do what Thou wilt with Me, but forgive them.

The answer came at once. God blotted out the handwriting of the decree that was against them with a pen dipped in His Son's Blood, and fastened it to the Cross. (Col. ii. 14.) The bill was paid, the sentence cancelled, the Ransom found. The Great Father forgave His children.

He still pleads my ignorance, for though I know more than the Jews did, I only "know in part." When I see Him face to face, I shall know far more, for "then I shall know even as I am known." (1 Cor. xiii, 12.) Then I shall, know for the first time what sin is, what *my* sin is; what it cost, and Who it was Who loved me enough to pay that cost; and I shall long to go and make one long Act of Contrition in "Purgatory's cleansing fires"; for though He has forgiven, and His Father has forgiven, I shall feel that I can never forgive myself.

Colloquy with Jesus, saying the first word on the Cross for me.

Resolution. To remember the lessons which the Hill of Calvary has brought before me today.

Spiritual Bouquet. "Father, forgive them, for they know not what they do."

Watchers on Calvary

Passion Week. Wednesday.

"And, they sat and watched Him." (St Matt. xxvii. 36).

1st Prelude. A picture of the crowd watching the Crucifixion.
2nd Prelude. Grace to be standing there too, doing what I can.

Point I.
They divided My garments among them (Ps. xxi. 19)

After the Cross had been raised up from the ground, and jolted into the hole prepared for it, the soldiers, seeing His clothes lying on the ground, hastened to divide them amongst themselves. St John says "they made four parts, to every soldier a part." Still, His coat remained, and there was evidently some thought of tearing this into four, and giving each a share; but even those rough, careless men thought it a pity to cut that woven, seamless tunic, which, tradition tells us, His Mother had made for Him when He was a baby, and which had grown with Him. It would be worth more whole than cut into four—this, no doubt, was their argument. And so they turned their thoughts from Him to busy themselves with His garments, as He prophesied that they would.

Let me see to it that I do not allow a little passing pleasure or gain, or following of my own will in any way, to turn away my thoughts from Jesus. Just for these last few days my mind and heart shall be fixed on the Cross where Jesus is dying for me. He Himself, and nothing less, shall be my portion.

Point II.

"All they that saw Me, laughed Me to scorn"

As soon as the Cross was lifted up, the mockery and derision began. All took part in it—"all they that saw Me"—the Rulers, the Chief Priests, the scribes, the elders, the soldiers, the mob, even the poor crucified thieves—all joined in—none had any pity. They wagged their heads, they blasphemed, saying: "Vah, Thou that destroyest the Temple of God, and in three days dost rebuild it, save Thy own self: if Thou be the Son of God, come down from the Cross." And it was the Chief Priests who added: "He saved others, Himself He cannot save; if He be the King of Israel, let Him now come down from the Cross, and we will believe in Him. He trusted in God, let Him now deliver Him, if He will have Him; for He said: I am the Son of God." (St Matt. xxvii. 39-43.)

Thus they mock and deride, while the Son of God is silently suffering and dying for them.

Is there anything I can do? It is hard to stand by and do nothing.

If, when people are saying hard things of me, I know there is someone standing by who believes none of them, who is angry at what is being said, who is looking at things entirely from my point of view, who is, in short, my friend, how much easier it is for me to bear it all! In a sense, what is being said by the others matters little. In a sense, the very calumnies are sweet to me, because I know that each one is drawing out fresh sympathy for me in the heart of my friend. That is the part Jesus expects me to play when I find myself amongst those who are saying hard things of Him, the part of a friend, of whose fidelity He is absolutely sure.

POINT III.

"AND THEY SAT AND WATCHED HIM"

Who were these watchers?

(1) There were those who watched from *duty*—the soldiers, who had to keep guard over their victim, and who were not allowed to leave till He was dead.

There are those who are watching during this Passion-tide simply from a sense of duty, or from habit. "It is Passion-week, and I must do something." Better to watch thus, than not at all.

(2) There were those who watched from *curiosity*—the crowd. Before the end came, their curiosity was changed into fear. "When they saw the things that were done, they were sore afraid." It was possibly that fear which bore fruit on the Day of Pentecost.

There are those who watch now, simply from curiosity. It may be the talk about some renowned preacher which arouses the curiosity, or the "Three Hours' Service," or the Passion Music. Let us pray that GOD will have pity on those who are watching even from lower motives, and that He will strike such fear into their hearts, as shall bring forth its fruit in due season.

(3) There were those who watched from *conviction*. Some of these returned home after all was over, striking their breasts. Amongst them was the Roman Centurion, a heathen. Every moment of that precious vigil was striking conviction into his heart. He had followed on the Way of the Cross; he had presided at the Crucifixion; he had heard the prayer: "Father, forgive them, for they know not what they do," and he knew that it was for him. By the time his watch is finished that prayer will be answered, and the Cross will

claim yet another captive, who will declare his allegiance by saying:"Indeed this Man was the Son of GOD."

And there are those in whose hearts conviction has been deepening while they have been watching this Lent. Let us pray GOD to finish the blessed work which He has begun in their hearts, so that they too may glorify Him by a good confession before Easter.

(4) There were those who watched *"afar off,"* because they were "anxious to see the end," though they dare not identify themselves too closely with their crucified Master, Amongst these was Peter, and probably some of his companions. They had been specially asked by their Master to watch. They are not doing it very bravely!

There are the fearful ones, too, amongst us today. They love their Master truly, but they watch "afar off." They dare not boldly acknowledge themselves on the aide of the Catholic Church. They dare not even cross the threshold of their Master's earthly home where the sacred drama is being enacted. Yet, in their heart of hearts, they do want "to see the end"; they are taking an intense interest in all that is going on; they want to be near their Master, and they envy those who are. The Heart of JESUS yearns to have them close to Him. What is it which keeps them "afar off"? GOD grant that this Passion-tide may bring grace and courage to these watchers, and that at Easter, when the Master pays His first visit, they may be found assembled, at any rate in spirit and intention, with the Church, over which Peter, the once fearful, now rules.

(5) Many ministering women also, who had been accustomed to follow Him, "stood afar off, beholding." Their mission had ever been to be somewhere in the background in case He needed their ministrations, and they are fulfilling it faithfully to the end.

Have these their counterpart today? To whom is this touching mission confided? Who are they who are waiting "afar off" in case their Master should want them? Surely they are His sick and suffering ones. They are somewhere in the background. *He* knows where, for it is His own detaining Hand, and not another's, which holds them at a distance. They have been "accustomed to follow" year by year, and they would fain join the faithful this year too, but He needs them in the background. There is work for them there, which only they can do. He needs their sufferings, and He needs their prayers, for which He has given them so much leisure. Who better than they, can aid Him in His great work? In reality they are nearer to Him than any, for they are stretched on the Cross with Him, "filling up those things that are wanting of the sufferings of Christ . . . for His Body, which is the Church" (Col. i. 24). If I am amongst these privileged ones, let me rejoice that I am "counted worthy to suffer"; let me value the mission confided to me; and remember that only one thing will enable me to fulfil it—keeping my eyes fixed on JESUS, and Him crucified.

(6) Lastly, there are some keeping their watch quite close to Him—His Mother; with John the beloved disciple; and Mary Magdalen, the queen of penitents.

This, unlike the last, is a group which all, who will, may join. Let me determine that this Passion-tide shall find me in that group—my hand in Mary's, and my heart full of love and penitence. I must not be surprised if, as soon as I have offered myself as a member of that inner circle, some fresh cross, which I had never suspected, is laid upon me. It is often so in Passion-tide; the Holy Mother experienced it. Those who take up their stand there mean Him to understand that He can count on them, and He takes them at their word.

Colloquy with JESUS, on the Cross.

Resolution. To get as near to the Cross as I can, regardless of consequences.

Spiritual Bouquet. "And the people stood, beholding." (St Luke xxiii. 35.)

— ❧ —

The Penitent Thief

Passion Week. Thursday.

"Amen, I say to thee, this day thou shalt be with Me in Paradise." (St Luke xxiii. 43.)

> 1ˢᵗ *Prelude.*   The three crosses.
> 2ⁿᵈ *Prelude.*   The grace of zeal for souls.

POINT I.
"WITH THE WICKED HE WAS REPUTED"

JESUS is dying. On either side of Him, dying also, a wretched robber is paying the penalty of his crimes. Together the three had been stretched on their crosses; together they had felt the piercings of the cruel nails. "With the wicked He was reputed." Suffering—intense suffering—for all the three! But how different were its effects! From the crosses of the thieves came shrieks of pain, mingled with curses and oaths; from the cross of JESUS a quiet, patient voice, praying that His enemies might be forgiven. How much suffering there is in the world! And how much of it is wasted! Let me always regard it as a precious gift from GOD, an opportunity for saying: "Not my will, but Thine"; an opportunity for crushing self;

for practicing patience, and meekness, and self-control. Let me regard it as something that I can offer in reparation for my sins, for the sins of others, for the conversion of sinners, and for all the intentions of His Sacred Heart. Here am I, Lord, helpless under Thy Hand which is striking me. I cannot *do* much, for I have been nailed to the cross by Thee, but I can *suffer* for Thee. I can offer to Thee all my sufferings, remembering that they have an expiatory value directly they are joined to the sufferings of Christ.

Now the crosses have been raised up, and the three victims are hanging where all may see them. Voices break the silence. Who is speaking? The two thieves are reproaching and reviling Jesus: "He trusted in God, let Him deliver Him if He will have Him, for He said: I am the Son of God." Words terrible enough on the lips of the soldiers and of the crowd, but far more terrible on the lips of dying men!

Point II.

The Conversion

Again the silence is broken, and one of the robbers calls out: "If Thou be the Christ, save Thyself and us!" This is meant as a blasphemy, not as a prayer. This time his companion does not join in; the precious moments that he has spent close to the Cross of Jesus have wrought a change in him; he no longer wants to revile Jesus; the light from the Cross has streamed into his dark soul, and he has seen himself, and everything else, in another light. He turns to show the light to his companion: "Neither dost thou fear God, seeing thou art under the same condemnation?" How strange these words of rebuke must have sounded in the ears of his companion! but how sweet in the ears of Him in whose defence he was speaking! During His whole lifetime Jesus had waited for that soul. His little leprous body had been cleansed by Him more than thirty years before, if the legend be true which tells us that when His Mother was fleeing into Egypt, she was offered shelter in a robbers' cave, and after she had washed her Holy Child, the robber's wife washed her baby in the same water, and lo! it was healed! Our Blessed Lord never works miracles on the body without the soul deriving some benefit. Was it the seed then sown in that little dark soul which, after having lain dormant for so long, was now springing up and bearing fruit? It may well have been so. What an incentive the thought should be to us to go on in faith sowing our seed in the hearts of His little ones. However unlikely the soil and the conditions, however impossible the surroundings, however much we may be tempted to think we are simply wasting our time, the seed is *there* with all its potentialities, waiting for the moment when the Cross of JESUS shall warm it into life and growth. This is probably the explanation of all sudden conversions.

But the dying thief has not finished yet. He has much to do, and the time is short. In the new light he sees the sins of his whole life, and he feels that he must confess them and get rid of them: "We indeed (are condemned) justly, for we receive the due reward of our deeds." Not many words, but how much is contained in them—a confession of his guilt, and an acknowledgment that he deserves punishment. Then he proclaims the innocence of JESUS: "This man hath done no evil." He feels the difference that there is between their lives and His, their, punishment and His. The light grows stronger still, it is turned full on to JESUS now, and the dying Penitent sees in this Innocent One all that he needs—his King and his GOD: "Lord, remember me," he cries, "when Thou comest into Thy Kingdom." How strong the light was! and how strong was his faith!

POINT III.

THE SECOND WORD FROM THE CROSS

At once comes the answer: "Amen I say to thee, this day thou shall be with Me in Paradise." What joy and peace these words must have brought to the dying thief! What a prospect—*with Him—in Paradise—today!* How quickly contrition and love touch the Heart of JESUS! I How richly He repays generosity! Not long after JESUS dies, and the thieves are left there—one, in spite of his wonderful opportunities, seeing JESUS die, and dying close to Him, with his heart steeled to the last; the other, with a wonderful calm and joy in his soul, waiting to go to his Savior, his Friend, his King and his GOD.

The second word was the outcome of the first: "Father, forgive them." His Father has already heard and answered. One soul for whom JESUS prayed has been forgiven.

What grace do we want to obtain from this Meditation? Surely the grace of zeal for souls; the grace to love the work for which our Master gave His life; to pray for sinners, especially during these last few days of Lent, to beg the Great Father to forgive them; to pray that, like the Penitent Thief, they may make a good confession before Easter. To be untiring in sowing the seed, believing that "we *shall* reap if we faint not"—perhaps never in this world, but most surely in the *Paradise* beyond, where we shall have the unspeakable joy of seeing *with Him* those in whose hearts we sowed the seed, those for whom we spent our health, our strength, our very lives. What will it matter then? Shall we regret it?

"It is the way the Master trod,
Shall not the servant tread it still? "

How much result was there of *His* work during His lifetime? Hardly any! "O Beloved Word of GOD, teach me to be generous—to give and not to count the cost, to fight and not to heed the wounds, to labor and not to ask for any reward save that of knowing that I do Thy Will."

> *Colloquy* with JESUS dying on the Cross for all those, about whose salvation I am anxious.

> *Resolution.* Never to despair of the salvation of any soul.

> *Spiritual Bouquet.* "This day thou shall be with Me in Paradise."

Stabat Mater

Feast of the Seven Dolours. Passion Week. Friday.

"There stood by the Cross of Jesus, His Mother. . . . When Jesus therefore had seen his Mother and the disciple standing, whom He loved, He saith to His Mother: Woman, behold thy son. After that, He saith to the disciple: Behold thy Mother. And from that hour the disciple took her to his own." (The "Gospel," St John xix. 26-27.)

> 1ˢᵗ *Prelude.* Mary standing at the Foot of the Cross.
> 2ⁿᵈ *Prelude.* The grace to stand there with her.

POINT I.
"THERE STOOD BY THE CROSS OF JESUS, HIS MOTHER"

The Church gives us this Feast before the "Great Week" begins, that we may learn how to suffer with JESUS, may meditate on the sufferings of Mary, and may remind ourselves that, through each step of the painful way, the *Passion* of JESUS and the *Com*-passion of Mary go hand in hand.

Mary *stood;* she had a sacrifice to offer, and she took the attitude of a sacrificing priest. Her holocaust was on the altar, about to be consumed. Mary had prepared her sacrifice beforehand—long years ago when she had consented to be the Mother of GOD. She had said her *Fiat* then, and she knew that it included Calvary. She accepted the gift that GOD then offered to her, knowing that she could only keep it till He asked it back from her. When her Child was forty days old Mary went to the Temple to present the Victim to GOD; just as, in the "Offertory" of the Mass, the Priest presents the host on the paten and the wine in the chalice, and the people present themselves to be offered in any way that GOD likes to choose. That day in the Temple was the day on which the first of the seven swords pierced the Mother's heart; for, though she knew the sorrow that awaited her, it pierced her through to hear it from the lips of another. Other sorrows in her life had kept constantly before her mind the fact that her Son was a Victim, and that one day she would have to offer Him up. When she fled with Him into Egypt she knew that her Child had enemies, and enemies who would one day hound Him to death. The joy of finding Him after the three days' loss was tempered by the thought that one day, as He said of Himself: "You shall seek Me, but you shall not find Me, because I go to the Father." Now His hour, and His Father's hour, had come. Mary had heard the cruel scourging; she had seen Him wearing the Crown of thorns, and being mocked as a King; she had met Him carrying His Cross as a criminal; she had seen Him fall under its weight from sheer exhaustion and pain; she had watched the people jeering, reviling, even spitting, upon her Son; she had heard the cruel nails being driven through those loved Hands and Feet. And now, her heart pierced with all these swords, she is standing at the Foot of the Cross—a *Valiant Woman,* indeed, offering her Son for the world's salvation.

What is the secret? How could any Mother, and especially the Mother of such a Son, bear all this? There is only one

WHAT MORE COULD I HAVE DONE FOR THEE, AND DID NOT DO? IT WAS I WHO OPENED A WAY FOR THEE THROUGH THE SEA: AND THOU HAST OPENED MY SIDE WITH A SPEAR. IT WAS I WHO BESTOWED UPON THEE A KINGLY SCEPTRE: AND THOU HAST SET UPON MY HEAD A CROWN OF THORNS. (Reproaches)

From the *Campion Missal and Hymnal*

answer. It was all GOD's Will, and GOD's Will was more precious to Mary than *anything* else. *Fiat mihi secundum, ver-
bum tuum.* These were the words that were on her lips and in
her heart. Here was her supernatural strength, enabling her
to bear each fresh thrust. And that supernatural strength is
not only for the Mother of GOD, it is for me too. It was not
because she was the Mother of GOD that she could bear all
her sorrows, but because she loved GOD's Will, because she
saw things from His point of view and not from her own—or
rather, she had made His point of view hers. Let me try to do
the same, and I shall be amazed at the courage, and strength,
and power of endurance that I possess.

POINT II.

"WOMAN, BEHOLD THY SON!"

As she stood there in the darkness with John, who, having come back from his cowardly flight, was doing his best
to protect her, her heart received another stab. It came from
the lips of her Son: "Woman," He said, looking down upon
her, "behold thy son!" How this word from the Cross must
have hurt her tender, loving heart! It meant, first, that she was
going to lose her own Son; then, that in His place she must
adopt another. We can realize something of what this must
have cost her, by thinking of the exquisite pain it gives us at
first to see others take, in any way, the place of those whom
we have lost—the title, the place at table, the room, the chair,
the duties. To see anything that belonged to them in the
hands of another opens the wound afresh. And yet none of
our loved ones can be to us what JESUS was to Mary. Now she
is asked to put John in the place of JESUS, "to exchange," as St
Bernard says, "the servant for the Lord! the disciple for the
Master! the son of Zebedee for the Son of GOD!"

Why did JESUS, Who loved His Mother far too much to spare her any suffering, pierce her heart with this particular sword? It was because He wanted her to see the whole human race represented in John. He was making her the Second Eve, the Mother of all living, and the pangs she was enduring were the pains of Motherhood. It was in her anguish at the Foot of the Cross that Mary won the right to call me her child. JESUS pierced Mary's heart that I might be a Child of Mary!

O holy Mother of GOD, behold your child! I am not worthy, but JESUS gave me to you. I am a part of His legacy; teach me to be all that a Child of Mary ought to be.

POINT III.

"BEHOLD THY MOTHER!"

The sword is still stabbing. Mary hears herself now being given away to another! Other lips than her Son's are to call her by the sweet name of Mother, But sorrow does not shrivel up Mary's Heart; on the contrary, it dilates it, and makes room in it for the great family which she now lovingly welcomes, as a parting gift from her Son—His family handed over to her so that she might take care of it for Him; "Take this child and nurse it for Me."

But how sweet must the words, that stabbed Mary's Heart, have been in the ears of the Beloved Disciple! His dear Lord and Master has already forgiven him his cowardice, and now is addressing one of His precious last words to him—he too is to have a legacy—*Behold thy Mother!* His Master has given him His own Mother to be *his* Mother! Could any legacy be more touching? Could He have left him anything dearer to His Own Heart? "From that hour the disciple took her to his own"—to his own home, to his own heart, to share everything that belonged to him, to make his interests hers, his friends hers, his very life hers.

But again, John was the representative of the whole human race. To me, no less than to him, was that precious legacy left. To me Jesus says: Behold thy Mother! Study her, love her, copy her, take her for your own, let her share everything that is yours.

What likeness is there between the child and the Mother? Do I try to be like her, in her love for Jesus, in her devotion to the cause for which He died, in her absolute submission to God's Will, in her patient suffering, in her looking at everything from God's point of view?

Holy Mary, Mother of God, and my Mother too, let me stand at the Foot of the Cross with you to learn its lessons and to learn how to be like the Mother of Sorrows.

Colloquy with Mary.

> *By the loved Cross with thee to stay,*
> *With thee to tread the painful way—*
> *Such is my fond desire!*

Resolution. To spend the remaining few days with Mary at the Foot of the Cross.

Spiritual Bouquet. "There stood by the Cross of Jesus, His Mother."

The Title of the Cross

Passion Week. Saturday.

"And Pilate wrote a Title[2] also: and he put it upon the Cross. And the writing was, JESUS of Nazareth, the King of the Jews." (St John xix. 19.)

1ˢᵗ Prelude. The INRI on a Crucifix (JESUS, Nazarenus, Rex Judæorum).
2ⁿᵈ Prelude. The grace to read it, and to understand it.

POINT I.
WHO WROTE THE TITLE?

Pilate wrote it. It was his duty as Procurator to write the name, the country, and the crime of the criminal. *Jesus,* of *Nazareth,* and His crime—that He was *King of the Jews.* And having written it, Pilate refused to alter it; though the Chief Priests, afraid that the people might believe that He *was* a King, begged him to do so. Do not put: The King of the Jews, but that: *He said,* I am the King of the Jews. "What I have written, I have written," answered Pilate doggedly. The Title, as it stood, set him free from the charge, which the Jews threatened to bring against him, of not being loyal to Cæsar. At any rate, if He *is* a King, I have crucified Him! And the Chief Priests had to be content. The Title, which had been nailed on over His Head, each blow of the hammer causing fresh agony to His tortured Body, and fresh pangs to the Heart of Mary, remained as Pilate had written it.

No, Pilate had no power to alter it, for it was the Holy Spirit Who had guided his hand to write that inscription. It proclaimed the royalty of JESUS, and no human hand had the power to touch that first piece of written revelation. How true are St Peter's words of every detail of the Passion: "Herod and

---

[2] The Title was found by St Helen and sent to Rome, where a precious fragment of it is still venerated in the Church of "The Holy Cross of Jerusalem."

Pontius Pilate with the Gentiles and people of Israel assembled together to do what *Thy Hand and Thy counsel decreed to be done*." (Acts iv. 18.)

If I am a follower of the Crucified One, this is no less true of my life than it was of His. Every detail, whether filled in by enemies or friends, is the fulfilling of God's decrees for me. He it is who guides the hands of all those who have anything to do with my life—and they can only do what He permits. How foolish, then, to want to alter anything! How shortsighted to complain and regret and rebel, and think I know better than God, Whose counsels are from all eternity! How puny are my ideas and plans for my welfare, compared with God's! Let me, as I stand beneath the Cross with Mary, reading the Title, determine that I will be a loyal subject of my King Who is hanging there—that is, that I will obey His slightest wish without any murmuring or questioning.

Point II.

For whom was the Title written?

For all. It was written in Hebrew, Greek, and Latin, that all might read and understand. "Many of the Jews read it." (John xix. 20.) Many, who had come from long distances to keep the Feast of the Passover at Jerusalem, read that the King of the Jews—perhaps their own Messias, for He was to be a King—was being crucified. Men of all nations were there; all instinctively would read the Title; all were talking about His Royalty. The Title was appealing to them from the Cross, teaching them the Name of Jesus, and inviting them to confess Him Lord of lords and King of kings. All was happening as the Chief Priests foresaw that it would, when they went and begged Pilate to put "*He said,*" before the incriminating words. "I, if I be lifted up, will draw all men to Myself." His word, were being fulfilled already.

Many are talking about Him this Lent. Many are being drawn closer to Him than they are, perhaps, during all the rest of the year. Let us pray that they, too, may be struck with the Royalty of Him Who hangs upon the Cross, and may make Him once and for all *their* King.

Point III.
What the Title means to me.

It contains three of the sweetest words I know—*Jesus*—*Nazareth*—*King,* and it is nailed to the *Cross.* Each word contains a mystery of love for me, for it was God, Who is love, Who wrote it:—

Jesus. My Savior, Who died for me.

Nazareth. What calm and peace and happiness the very word brings with it! What memories it calls up! How full to overflowing must the Heart of Mary have been as she read the words over her dying Son: Jesus of *Nazareth*! Which of the virtues is not recalled by the word!—hiddenness, poverty, obedience, patience, charity, humility, self-sacrifice. It is at the school of Nazareth that all these are to be learned.

King. King of kings—yes, but my King, mine to serve, to copy, to love, to be faithful to, always, and in every place, "In what place soever my Lord the King is, there will also Thy servant be." My King is on the Cross, that is why His servant is standing at the Foot.

Each of these three words is nailed to the *Cross.* Each is inseparable from the Cross. Each draws all its virtue from the Cross. If I am to have a share in these words, I must have a share also in the Cross. "Unless a man take up his cross and follow Me, he cannot be My disciple." He cannot say the sweet Name of JESUS; he cannot understand, much less learn, the virtues of Nazareth; and it is impossible for him to serve a King Who reigns from the Cross.

Colloquy with JESUS, thanking Him for the Title, which love wrote "over His Head."

Resolution. To read the Title many times today.

Spiritual Bouquet. "JESUS of Nazareth, King of the Jews."

— ❧ —

The Triumph of the King

𝕻𝖆𝖑𝖒 𝕾𝖚𝖓𝖉𝖆𝖞.

"Rejoice greatly, O daughter of Sion, shout for joy, O daughter of Jerusalem. Behold, thy King will come to thee, the just and Savior: He is poor; and riding upon an ass, and upon a colt the foal of an ass." (Zach. ix.9.)

> 1st *Prelude.*   Any picture of Christ riding into Jerusalem.
> 2nd *Prelude.*   The grace to be loyal.

We must turn our eyes away from the Cross today, for Holy Church would have her children fix their minds, not on their King dying, but on their King riding in triumph, surrounded by His loyal, rejoicing subjects. In our Meditation yesterday it was the pagan Pontius Pilate who proclaimed the kingly character of the Crucified. Today it is His own people, the Jews, who pay Him royal homage, and the Church bids us all join in, and find consolation in the midst of our sorrow, by going out to meet our King, singing Hosannahs, and carrying in our hands the palms of victory—even when "the Passion" is being read, and offering them to Him as a protest against the outrages He suffered, and as a sign of joy and

AND JESUS FOUND A YOUNG ASS, AND SAT UPON IT, AS IT IS WRITTEN: FEAR NOT, DAUGHTER OF SION: BEHOLD, THY KING COMETH, SITTING ON AN ASS'S COLT. THESE THINGS HIS DISCIPLES DID NOT KNOW AT THE FIRST; BUT WHEN JESUS WAS GLORIFIED, THEN THEY REMEMBERED THAT THESE THINGS WERE WRITTEN OF HIM. (John 12)

From the *Campion Missal and Hymnal*

thanksgiving for the victory He gained for us over sin and death and hell.

Point I.
The King's Needs

"*The Lord hath need of them.*" It is my King Who is speaking. He wants something. He wants to show Himself as a King. He wants to fulfil the ancient prophecy, by riding in triumph into Jerusalem. But He has made Himself poor for the sake of His people; He has made Himself dependent upon them. He cannot carry out His purposes without their help.

"*The Lord hath need of them.*" My King has made Himself dependent for my sake. More than this, He has made Himself dependent on *me*. He wants to ride in triumph over His enemies in my heart, and He sends a message asking for my cooperation: *The Lord hath need* of that particular corner of your heart which is occupied. He has need of the love which is lawfully His and which is being given to another. *The Lord hath need* of that treasured possession, for which you have worked and toiled perhaps for a lifetime. *The Lord hath, need* of your health, of your strength, of your wealth. *The Lord hath need* of that particular talent; He knows that, to all appearance, it is being used for Him, but He says that all the glory and praise are not being passed on to Him. *The Lord hath need* of this other talent to be laid entirely on one side for His sake. He knows how difficult it will be for you to understand this, because you have always been so proud to use it in His service, and it will seem to you that you can never do anything for Him without it. But He would have you understand that one of His reasons for giving it you was that you might have something really *costly* to offer to Him, something which will be a substantial help to Him in His work in your heart, a sacrifice which will lay self so low, that His march of triumph there will be comparatively easy.

And the more complete the triumph has been in my heart, the more help will He expect from me in His work in the hearts of others. All these souls that He is out to conquer! Is He going to the battle alone? No, again He has made Himself dependent on His creatures. He sends His messengers saying: *The Lord hath need* of you—need of the very things He gave you when He took possession of your heart, and made it His munition store. His weapons of warfare "are not carnal"—they are these: humility, patience, love, zeal, perseverance, talents—perhaps the very one that it cost so much to lay aside once. All these, gained with so much labor and effort, with such anguish and so many tears, when the battle was being fought and won in your own heart, *the Lord* now *has need of,* and He calls upon you to use them for Him in His great offensive against the enemy.

Thy King, then, has need of much that I can give Him. He is continually sending His messengers for one thing or another. Some are poor and needy; others ignorant, sick, sorrowing; some are tired and overburdened; some are sinful; and many are uncongenial. What tact the King's messengers require! Do I always treat them with the dignity that they deserve? Do I give them of my best—of the Royal Bounty which the King has entrusted to me? Is He sure that, however inconvenient the time may be when His messengers arrive, and however difficult or distasteful their request, He has only to say: "The Lord *has need* of it," and straightway I shall loose it and let it go? If not, there is something defective about my loyalty, and Palm Sunday has a word of warning for me.

Point II
The King's Triumph

The people are full of hope and expectation. All do something to make the royal ride a success. Some give the ass, some fetch it, some make a saddle, some take off their garments and make a carpet of them, some cut down branches of trees and strew them in His path, some wave their palms and cry: *Hosannah in the Highest;* all except the jealous Pharisees, join in the cry of welcome: "Blessed be the King Who cometh in the Name of the Lord, peace in Heaven, and glory on high." (St Luke xix. 38.)

It was an undoubted triumph; "the whole city was moved," and the Scribes and Pharisees were very anxious; and even asked Our Lord to stop the shouts of praise: "Master, rebuke Thy disciples." But He shamed them with the answer: "If these hold their peace, the stones will cry out." Praise *must* be given; you Pharisees will not give it; if the people do not, who will?

Someone must acknowledge Christ's royalty. The question for me to answer today, as I receive and carry my palm, is: Am I going to be the one, or am I going to leave it to others? It is my King riding there, riding on to, die for me! Is it possible for me to do anything else but praise Him, that is, approve of all He does—of all His dealings with me, giving Him cheerfully all that He asks, anxious for His triumph to be complete over every corner of my heart? Is it possible that there is even today something in my life over which I do not wish *Him* to reign? Over which I would rather—at any rate for the present—keep the government in my own hands? If so His triumph is not yet complete, and I am siding with the Pharisees, thinking things are going a little too far! As I look at my palm, let me remember that though it means victory, the victory has to be gained, as my King gained His, through much suffering. "I must decrease"—there is the suffering. "He must increase"—there is the triumph.

Point III.
The King's Tears

There *are* those who fail Him, "O Jerusalem, behold thy King cometh to thee." "And when He drew near seeing the city, He wept over it." He could not ride there in triumph. He had failed to gain their hearts. He had tried during these last three years, but there had been no cooperation, no giving to Him of the things He needed and asked for. "If thou hadst known," there would never have been a deicide! Why did they not know? Because they deliberately closed their hearts against Him; they would not hear of the things that belonged to their peace; and now it was too late—they were hidden from their eyes. No wonder He wept. He loved the city; it was His own. "How often would I have gathered you, but *you would not.*"

If the King cannot triumph over hearts, He must weep over them. Let me think about this, and ask myself which it has been in *my* heart? Have I never been fickle? full of good resolutions, which were so easily broken? swayed by the company I happened to be in, whether it cried *Hosannah* or *Crucify Him*? For me happily it is not too late, I have still time to dry His tears by letting mine flow. Let me promise Him on this Palm Sunday, when He is expecting my homage, that never again will I say to Him: Thus far shall Thou go, and no farther; this is *my* ground, *I* reign here! Let me tell Him that from henceforth I intend to have done with all fickleness, so that He may be able to count on my Hosannahs, and not have to weep because He knows that they will soon give place to cries of Crucify Him!

Colloquy with my King.

Resolution. To be really loyal.

Spiritual Bouquet. "The Lord hath need of them."

— ❧ —

Events of the Day for Contemplation

Palm Sunday.

1. JESUS, leaving His Mother with Lazarus and his sisters, sets forth from Bethany.
2. He sends two of His disciples for the ass and her colt.
3. He rides in triumph into Jerusalem.
4. Beholding the city, He weeps over it.
5. In the evening He goes back to Bethany. No one offers Him hospitality in the city. Jerusalem has received her King with acclamations, but she has neither food, nor rest, nor shelter to offer Him.

Desolation and Thirst

Holy Week. Monday.

"Turn not away Thy Face from Thy servant. . . . In My thirst they gave Me vinegar to drink." (Ps. lxviii. 18, 22.)

1ˢᵗ *Prelude.* The Foot of the Cross.
2ⁿᵈ *Prelude.* The grace to realize the excess of His love.

POINT I.
THE DARKNESS

Two hours or more have elapsed since JESUS willed away His only remaining possession—His Mother. The end is drawing near now. For nearly three hours JESUS has been hanging on the Cross. For nearly three hours Mary has bravely stood at her post. Darkness—thick darkness—has enshrouded everything, and has created a silence which was intense. Some of the people have, perhaps, managed to grope their way home, but terror roots most of them to the spot. Long ago the jeers and the blasphemies have died away. Even the soldiers' dice are silent—they cannot continue their games in the dark. What does it all mean? It means that JESUS, the GOD-Man, is dying—dying at the hands of His own creatures—and that the Sun refuses to shine on a deed so heinous—Nature herself revolts. But it means more than this, Why is the God-Man dying? He, the Just, is dying for the unjust. He is paying the penalty of sin. He is satisfying His Father's justice. He is bearing the full weight of His Father's anger; and in consequence, His Father's Face is averted. "Him that knew no sin, for us He hath made sin," (2 Cor. v. 21), and the All-Holy, All-Just, cannot look upon sin. He refuses to look upon His own Beloved Son, No wonder the world was dark! GOD was hiding His Face! It is a mystery, and the more we meditate about it, the more we feel that it is beyond us; but this much of it we may understand—GOD refused at that moment of moments to look upon the Face of His Son, in order that we, from henceforth, might always be able to say in our prayers: "Look, O Lord, upon the Face of Thine Anointed," confident that, looking, He would be bound to grant our requests. GOD turned away His Face from JESUS that He might never turn it away from those for whom He was dying.

POINT II.

THE ABANDONMENT

What has JESUS been doing all this time? What have been His thoughts? Ah! who shall say? They are too deep for words. Something of the depression which He felt in the Garden is upon Him; and suddenly in the midst of the silence and darkness He cries out with a loud voice, "My GOD, My GOD, why hast Thou forsaken Me?" His Father had forsaken Him in anger, and He knew that His anger was just. Verily, He is drinking His chalice to the dregs! Such is the bitterness of His Soul, that He does not use the word "*Father.*" "My GOD, My GOD." A GOD of justice, a GOD afar off, a GOD Who hides Himself.

This terrible agony of soul, my JESUS, Thou didst endure for me. Thou, Who wouldst be tried in all things as we are, didst go to the very brink of hell. Only the Souls in Hell really know what it is to be abandoned by GOD. To them He has said: Depart *from Me*. It is the pain of loss—the loss of GOD— the greatest of all Hell's terrible pains—the pain which makes hell. It was that I might never hear this terrible sentence that Thou, my JESUS, didst suffer Thine abandonment.

As I stand at the Foot of the Cross with Mary, and listen to that cry of anguish coming from the depths of His broken Heart, let me try to realize something of the excess of

His love. And when sometimes God seems to hide His Face from me for a little moment, and I have to pass through the dark waters of *desolation,* let me never lose confidence nor hope. He is only allowing me to share a little of the mental agony of Jesus—only taking me at my word and allowing me to be where my King is. And let me remind Him, and myself too, that He forsook His dear Son, in order that He might *never* forsake me.

Point III.

The Thirst

Nearly all things have been accomplished—there is just one more prophecy to be fulfilled: "And Jesus, knowing that all things were now accomplished that the Scripture might be fulfilled, said: I thirst." He cannot die till He has fulfilled every jot and tittle that was prescribed for Him. What a lesson for those who find attention to detail trying, and who are disposed to think that little things do not matter.

This word from the Cross followed closely on the last, even while the bystanders, relieved by the dispersing darkness, were venturing to begin again their mockery. "*Eli, Eli.* He calleth for Elias. Let us see if Elias will come to take Him down." At His word "one ran with a sponge filled with vinegar, and putting it on a reed, gave Him to drink." And He tasted it. One more pang added to His sufferings, even at the last moment, was welcome to Him. Besides, there was the Prophecy: "In My thirst, they gave Me vinegar to drink."

One of the most excruciating of all the pains of crucifixion is the intolerable thirst, caused by the loss of blood from so many wounds. In the case of Jesus, this was intensified by the fact that He had taken nothing. He had refused the mixture of myrrh offered Him just before the crucifixion. He had probably had nothing to drink since He drank of the cup at the Last Supper. And Mary heard her Son say: *I thirst,* and watched the bitter, nauseous drink being handed to Him, and she could do nothing. It was only another stab piercing her Heart, to be borne in silence and in union with His sufferings.

But it was not only the Prophecy, still less was it His Own physical suffering, that JESUS was thinking of now. He was gathering up into that one word "*Sitio,*" the whole of His life and death. He was gathering up all His intentions, and pouring out His whole soul to His Father. He was thirsting for the salvation of souls, for the Redemption of the world, for the accomplishment of His Father's Will, for the increase of His glory.

"*I thirst.*" At that moment He saw my soul, and He thirsted for it. He knew all about it—its fickleness, its treachery, its carelessness and indifference. He saw all its dangers, difficulties, and temptations. He saw how near it would be to actual ruin, and He said: Father, *I thirst* for that soul, I want it, I love it, give it Me. And the Father heard His cry, and quenched His thirst to the full, giving Him the souls for whom He was shedding His Blood, and satisfying His cravings to such an extent that it mattered little to Him what the man with the sponge and the vinegar and the reed was doing, nor what the bystanders were saying.

> *Colloquy.* O my JESUS, as I stand at the Foot of the Cross with Thy sweet Mother, I promise Thee that I will cooperate with that Thirst of Thine, that I will give Thee what Thou wert thirsting for— my *love.* And that I will, by my untiring zeal for souls, ever seek to quench Thy Thirst.

> *Resolution.* Never to forsake Him, and never refuse to quench His thirst.

> *Spiritual Bouquet.* "I thirst. Give Me to drink."

— ✥ —

Events of the Day for Contemplation

Monday in Holy Week.

1. JESUS goes again from Bethany to Jerusalem with His disciples.
2. He is hungry, and curses the fig-tree, which bore leaves but no fruit. (St Matt. xxi. 18-20.) He is thinking of the picture of Jerusalem rather than of His own hunger.
3. He cleanses the Temple, and then spends most of His day there, healing the blind and the lame, and holding conversations with the Priests and Elders. (St Matt. xxi.)
   The little children, catching sight of Him in the Temple, and remembering yesterday's joy, begin again their Hosannahs.
4. The Chief Priests in the Palace are seeking how they may destroy Him. (St Mark xi.)
5. At even-tide, He goes out of the city, into Bethany, with the twelve. (St Mark xi. 11.)

"Consummatum est"

Holy Week. Tuesday.

"When Jesus, therefore, had taken the vinegar, He said: It is consummated." (St John xix. 30.)

1st *Prelude.*   Jesus on the Cross—the last moments.
2nd *Prelude.*   Grace to understand.

Point I.
The Artists

"It is consummated." Every type and prophecy has been fulfilled. Every "jot and tittle" has been supplied; Jesus is free, now, to die.

For four thousand years the artists had been at work, each representing some part of the great picture. Now it is finished. Did Jesus think of them all when He said: *Consummatum est*? Did He think of *Adam* and *Eve* being consoled by the promise of a Savior? Did He think of *Abraham,* who rejoiced to see His day? Of *Job,* who gained courage from the thought of his "Redeemer"? Of *Moses,* who told of the "Great Prophet" that was to come? Of *Balaam's* prophecy of His "Star"? Of *David,* who never tired of singing of the Messias—of His Passion and Resurrection? Of *Isaias,* who prophesied of His sweet Mother, and of His Virgin Birth, and who wrote so tenderly of His sufferings? Of *Daniel,* who counted the years till His coming, so intense were his desires? Of *Micheas,* who pointed out the very town where He, whose "going forth was from the days of eternity," was to be born? Of *Aggeus,* who said that the "Desired of all nations" should come and fill the new temple with glory? Of *Zacharias,* who bid Jerusalem shout for joy because her King was coming to her? Of *Malachias,* who spoke of the

Forerunner who was to prepare His way? Did He think of them all? In less than three days He will Himself be pointing out these prophecies and many others to two of His disciples, and showing them how many "things concerning Himself" lie hidden in the Scriptures, and that He could not have been the Messias had He not been able to say of them: "*Consummatum est.*"

But the *types* as well as the prophecies were included in His "*Consummatum est.*" Did the Lamb of God think of all the millions of lambs whose deaths on the Jewish altars had foreshadowed His death on the Cross? Did the Great Antitype think of *Adam,* the father of all? Of *Abel,* whose offering was accepted by God, but who was nevertheless slain by his brother? Of *Noe,* who saved his people in the ark? Of *Melchizedek,* King and Priest, who brought forth bread and wine? Of *Isaac,* who carried the wood upon which he was to be offered? Of *Joseph,* who was sold and put into prison by his brethren, and who afterwards sustained their lives by giving them bread? Of *Moses,* who delivered his people from bondage? Of *Elias,* who fasted forty days and forty nights, and who went up by a whirlwind into Heaven? Of *David,* the man after God's own heart, who, single-handed, met the foe that threatened to overthrow the armies of Israel? Of *Solomon,* who built the temple? Of *Jonas,* who was three days and three nights in the fish?

"*Consummatum est.*" Stand back now all you that have been painting His picture. It is finished, and it is *perfect*—so perfect that the people recognize it, and say: "Is not this the Christ?" "This is indeed He." "Indeed this was the Son of God."

Point II.
The Picture

"*Consummatum est.*" The picture is finished. All the different parts have been collected into one whole—Jesus, Prophet, Priest, and King, the Savior of the world. It is the death of Jesus which has put the finishing touch to the picture—it has put His seal to it, and stamped it as His Own. How?

(1) *By His sufferings*—mental and physical. He has drained the bitter cup to the dregs. Thirty-three years He has lived on the earth, and they have been years of hard work, poverty, isolation, humiliation, misunderstanding. Every detail foretold of His sufferings has been fulfilled.

(2) *By the Redemption of the world.* "I have finished the work which Thou gavest Me to do." The ransom has been paid, the reconciliation between God and man effected, the slaves set free. Every drop of His Blood has been poured out as an offering to His Father, for the guilty children of Adam. There is nothing more to be done, it *is* finished; and in return He demands a general pardon.

(3) *By His victory over Satan.* Satan has found out at last Who He is. The question is no longer an undecided one. No need for any more battles now; Jesus is the Conqueror, the human race belongs to Him. "By death He has destroyed him that had the empire of death, that is, the devil." (Heb. ii. 14.) And by the finishing touch of Jesus, Satan is blotted out of the picture for ever, "*Consummatum est.*"

"What more could I have done that I have not done?"

Point III

A COPY

All artists like to copy the *best* pictures. Jesus is my model, and I must try to copy Him. It would seem a task more hopeless than setting a little child down before one of the Great Masters and bidding him make a copy, were it not that directly He sees my desire and goodwill He comes Himself to my aid, and saying encouragingly: "Without Me you can do nothing," He guides my unskillful fingers till some sort of likeness to Himself is produced.

As I stand at the Foot of the Cross today and hear Him say, *"Consummatum est,"* I cannot but think of the moment when my soul, too, must go back to Him Who gave it, to give an account of the work He has given me to do. O my Jesus, out of gratitude to Thee I should like, at that moment, to be able to copy Thee, and to say, in my little measure: It is finished. How can I? There is only one way, My child, of ensuring it: be faithful to the grace of the present moment, see to it that each thing you have to do, each word that you say, every breath that you draw, every beat of your heart, is for God—all to give Him pleasure. I did always the things which pleased Him, and so I could say: It is finished. Let your Examinations of Conscience be rigid on this point. Have I today done the work He has given me to do? and has my motive in doing it been to please God? Do not be afraid, My child, I finished all for you. Shoulder your cross and mount with Me the hill of Calvary, there allow yourself to be nailed to it, bravely resist all the cries that tell you to "come down from the cross," and you too will be pleasing to My Father, and be able at the end to say: It is finished. The secret of this word, *Consummatum est,* is *sacrifice.* Only by the sacrifice of *self* can you be to GOD as a sweet-smelling savor, and fulfil the task Heh given you to do.

    Colloquy with JESUS on the Cross.

    Resolution. To do today something that will help me to say: "Consummatum est," at the last.

    Spiritual Bouquet. "Consummatum est."

Events of the Day for Contemplation

Tuesday in Holy Week.

1. They come again from Bethany to Jerusalem. The disciples notice the fig-tree "dried up by the roots," and receive a lesson on faith and prayer.

2. He goes into the Temple, and is asked by the Chief Priests: "By what authority" He is doing these things. He puzzles them by asking them a question about the Baptism of John. He then tells His Parables, (St Matt. xxi.), which annoy the Chief Priests, (St Luke xx. 19), and they hold another Council to see how they can ensnare Him in His speech. As a result all try to do so—the Pharisees, the Herodians, the Sadducees—and not only does He answer all their puzzling questions, so that the multitudes are in admiration at His doctrine, but also, He asks them such a puzzling question that no man can answer it, and thus effectually silences them. (St Matt. xxii.)

3. He gives His last public discourses in the Temple, (St Matt. xxiii.), and as He comes out, sits over against the Treasury, and notices how the people give their alms. (St Mark xii. 41.)

4. In the evening He sets out again for Bethany. On the way He sits for a while on the Mount of Olives, and the disciples ask Him when this terrible vengeance, about which He has been telling the Jews, will come. He says, when the measure of iniquity is full; and for the destruction of Jerusalem He fixes the time: "This generation shall not pass till all be fulfilled." (St Matt. xxiv.)

5. He joins His friends in Bethany.   (Bethany was situated on the slope of Olivet.)

The Ninth Hour

"And Jesus crying with a loud voice, said: Father, into Thy Hands I commend My spirit, and, bowing His Head, He gave up the ghost." (St Luke xxiii. 46; St John xix. 30.)

> 1st *Prelude.*   Jesus on the Cross—the last moment.
> 2nd *Prelude.*   The grace *to die well.*

POINT I.
HIS DEATH

"JESUS again crying with a loud voice." (St Matt. xxvii. 50.) This is to draw the attention of the bystanders to the fact that the Son of GOD is not dying from weakness or exhaustion, but because it is His Will to die. "No man taketh (My life) away from Me: but I lay it down of Myself, and I have power to lay it down." (St John x. 18.) He is now exercising that power.

"And bowing His Head." What calm majesty there is in this action! Again, no weakness is here. It is the deliberate act of one who has waited till the right moment has come. He bows His Head to His Father in a farewell greeting, as one who, having given an account of his commission, bows himself out from the presence of the King.

"Father, into Thy hands I commend My spirit." His last words, as His first, are for His Father. His first recorded words are: "I must be about My Father's business." And between the two: "My meat is to do the Will of Him Who sent Me, that I may perfect His work." (St John iv. 34.) *Father.* He has found Him again now. He is no longer a GOD of justice; the peace

has been sealed. *Into Thy Hands,* till the Resurrection. *I commend My spirit,* My human soul which Thou createdst. It was a precious treasure, and He put it into the safe keeping of His Father's Hands. He made, in other words, the sacrifice of His life, and once more His Father was well pleased.

"*He gave up the ghost.*" Just one more thing He has to do—*to die,* to give His soul leave to quit His Body. It is all over now. The Shepherd has laid down His life for His sheep. His excess of love has found its vent in His death.

Let me learn of JESUS how to die. I need "fear no evil" when the last moment comes for me. JESUS has passed that way before me, and by "tasting death for all," (Heb. ii. 9), has robbed it of its terrors. He will Himself be waiting to take me through the dark valley. Let me learn from Him how pleasing to GOD is the sacrifice of my life, and let me give Him this pleasure often. I cannot, as JESUS did, decide the moment for myself, but I can say: When the moment, already decided by Thee, comes, O Lord, take my life as the homage due to Thee. I make the sacrifice of it *now,* that there may be no mistake about it. "Father, into Thy Hands I commend my spirit."

POINT II.

MIRACLES OF NATURE AND GRACE

The Jews who were assembled in the Temple for the Feast had a terrible shock at that momentous ninth hour, for suddenly the veil of the Temple, which for so long had hid from their view the awful Holy of Holies, was rent in two from the top to the bottom! Exposed to public view were "the Cherubim of glory, overshadowing the Propitiatory," (Heb. ix. 5), which none but the High Priest had ever been allowed to see, and he only once a year. According to an old tradition, the Angels were heard to say, as they hurried out of the Temple:

"Let us go hence! Let us go hence! The Holy of Holies is no more!" What did this miracle mean? The Jews did not understand—and they do not even now—that it meant that the Messias was come, and that, by His death. He had fulfilled all the law. The Old Dispensation was gone for ever."

But this was not the only miracle. That Ninth Hour made itself felt in Heaven as well as on earth, in Limbo, in Purgatory, and even in Hell. Nature was proclaiming that He, Who had been crucified, was her GOD; the Sun again gave his light, the earth trembled and the rocks were rent. Tradition says that a great chasm opened between the Cross of JESUS and that of the impenitent thief. In Purgatory many souls were released to meet their Savior in Limbo; and many of the just souls from Limbo were about to be sent to rejoin their bodies—the graves were already opening, and when the Master rose from the dead, "many saints arose" too. And in Hell, the Prince of darkness was trembling; his hour was come—the hour which he had expected ever since his direful curse in Eden. His head had now been crushed, his power taken away. "The devils also believe, and tremble." (Jas. ii. 19.) He believed now, and he trembled, and all Hell with him.

But grace was busy with her miracles, too, at this marvellous ninth hour. The Centurion, struck by the loud cry, and terrified by the earthquake, was at last convinced, and cried out before everyone: "Indeed this Man was the Son of GOD," as though he had been thinking it possible all along, but now he has the proof. His soldiers caught up his words—words which proclaimed His Divinity, His Humanity and His innocence—and miracles of grace were worked in many a dark, heathen heart. But the Jews were not outdone by the Gentiles: "All the multitude of them that were come together to that sight, and saw the things that were done, returned, striking their breasts."

To strike the breast is to say: "Mea culpa," and this is a miracle of grace.

The age of miracles is not passed. As I stand at the Foot of the Cross today, I want to plead specially for some for whom I have pleaded, seemingly in vain, for years. Often I have been tempted to give up and to say: "It is no use." May this Meditation on Thy death, and on these miracles of grace worked in the most unlikely hearts, quicken me to fresh effort, O my Jesus. "Thy Hand is not shortened that it cannot save." Once more I plead for that soul. Thou lovest it. Thou didst die for it. Work yet another miracle of grace.

POINT III.

Pilate and his Messages

Much has happened since we last saw Pilate, though in point of time it is only three or four hours ago. Who can say what his thoughts have been during those long hours? Whatever they were, two sets of messengers now break in upon them:—

(1) The Jews, scrupulous about not breaking their Sabbath, were beginning to get anxious. Only three hours now before it began, and they did not want to have it desecrated by the bodies being left hanging on the crosses, so they besought Pilate that the legs of the criminals might be broken to hasten death, and then the bodies could be taken down and buried before the Sabbath began. Pilate. granted their request, and despatched soldiers for the purpose.

(2) Joseph of Arimathea, a secret disciple, had been busy making his plans. He, too, knew that there was no time to be lost if he was to carry them out. He had been thinking of the new tomb that had been cut in the rock for himself, and had made up his mind to give it to his Master. He was "a good and a just man," and wanted to make what reparation he could

for his half-heartedness. Though a member of the Sanhedrin, "he had not consented to their counsel and doings." He "had been looking for the kingdom of GOD," and his vigil by the Cross had taught him much about that kingdom. He had seen its King die, and had resolved that from henceforth he would be a member of the kingdom. No more secret discipleship for him! "He went in *boldly* to Pilate, and begged the Body of JESUS," for he could not bear the thought of its being left to the mercy of the soldiers. Pilate kept him waiting for his answer, for "he wondered that He should be already dead," he had only just sent soldiers to break His legs. He must be sure that there was no trickery here; he was not going to give permission to take Him down till he was certain of His death. He sent for the Centurion, and asked him whether it was true that He was "already dead." Ah! the Centurion could tell him! Did he tell him, too, what an awful mistake he had made—that it *was* the Son of GOD whom he had crucified? "Then Pilate commanded that the Body should be delivered to Joseph." What a joy for him! and what a sense of responsibility must have possessed his "noble" soul!

While these messengers are going to and fro to the Governor's house, Mary is still standing at the Foot of the Cross. John is there too, for he cannot leave her. Mary Magdalen is still in her loved place kneeling at His Feet. The little groups of women are still watching. The two thieves are still living; the loud cry and the gaping chasm in the rock beneath them have been powerless, either to touch the hard heart of the one, or to disturb the deep peace of the other.

Let me linger there still with Mary, for the Hypostatic union can never be broken; while the Human Soul of JESUS accompanied by the Divinity has gone to Limbo, the Divinity remains also with the lifeless Body. My GOD is still hanging on the Cross.

Colloquy with Mary about all that has happened during this ninth hour.

Resolution. To recall the ninth hour often today.

Spiritual Bouquet. "Father, into Thy Hands I commend My spirit."

— ⚜ —

Events of the Day for Contemplation

Wednesday in Holy Week.

1. Our Lord seems to have spent, all this day either in Bethany or in some other part of the Mount of Olives. It was the last day He would spend entirely with His friends—the Holy Women, His Disciples, His Apostles, His Mother.

2. He tells the Parables of the Ten Virgins, the Talents, and the Last Judgment. (St Matt. xxv.)

3. An important Council was held today in the High Priests' Palace. Its object was to see how they could get rid of Jesus. Was it prudent to take steps just now, when Jerusalem was full of visitors, and just after the enthusiasm of Sunday? Would it not be better to wait till after the Feast? The Divine decrees had fixed the hour—it was to be *during* the Feast.

4. Judas came into the Council with a proposition: "What will you give me, and I will deliver Him unto you?" It was just what they wanted; the agreement was soon made, "they covenanted with him for thirty pieces of silver.

— ❦ —

The Memorial of His Passion

Maundy Thursday.

"The Lord JESUS, the same night in which He was betrayed, took bread, and giving thanks, broke and said: Take ye and eat: this is My Body which shall be delivered for you: this do for the commemoration of Me. In like manner also the chalice, after He had supped, saying: This chalice is the New Testament in My Blood; this do ye, as oft as you shall drink, for the commemoration of Me." (From the "Epistle," 1 Cor. xi. 23-25.)

1st Prelude.   Mass on Maundy Thursday.
2nd Prelude.   Grace to remember, and be thankful.

Today is a day of many memories, but the two to which the Church gives the greatest prominence are the Betrayal, and the Institution of the Holy Eucharist. Those who follow carefully the Liturgy for today, will continually be reminded of the former; but it is out of gratitude for the latter that the Church bids all hearts and voices join in an outburst of thanksgiving, and allows the Mass to be celebrated with all possible solemnity, though we are in the midst of Holy Week. Although she reserves for the Feast of Corpus Christi a still more solemn honoring of the great Gift bestowed today, and though she may not yet sing her Alleluias, still the Maundy Thursday Mass has a solemnity all its own. The organ is let loose again; the candles are lighted; the altar is decorated; white vestments are worn; the crucifix and statues, though still veiled, have laid aside their mourning; the *Gloria in ecccelsis* is heard once more, and then, the Rubric says, "the bells are rung." And, as if to make up for the silence that is coming, every bell makes "a joyful noise." Did the Church choose the Hymn which the Angels sang at His Birth as the signal for the ringing of joy bells, because we are honoring today the great Sacrament which is the extension of the Incarnation? After the *Gloria,* the bells are silent, even at the *Elevation,* reminding us that our joy must be tempered, we must not forget that it is *Holy Week.* In yet one more way the Church shows that this is indeed a Feast which she delights to honor, and that is, by permitting three changes in the *Canon* of the Mass. On a few other Great Festivals she allows one or other of the two first, and sometimes (at Easter and Pentecost) *both.* But Maundy Thursday is the only day on which a *third,* is permitted. Our Meditation will help us to keep in the spirit of the Church, if we take the additional words which constitute the three changes, as our three points.

POINT I.

THE "COMMUNICANTES"

The moment the *Gloria in excelsis* is finished, and the joyous bells have ceased, the Church reminds us in the *"Collect"* that it cannot be *all* joy today, because it is the Anniversary also of the *Betrayal.* The words are almost startling, for it is such a sudden change after the outburst of praise: "O God, from Whom *Judas received the punishment of his guilt."* In the *"Epistle"* comes another reminder: "The Lord JESUS, *the same night in which He was betrayed,* took bread." The *"Gospel"* tells us that "the devil put it into the heart of Judas Iscariot, the son of Simon, *to betray Him."* Then when the *"Preface" of the Cross* has ushered in the *"Canon"* of the Mass, and we get to the part *"Within the Action,"* we come to the first change—that in the prayer beginning *"Communicantes":* "Communicating *and celebrating the most sacred day in which our Lord JESUS Christ was delivered up."* (Traditus est.) We should have expected, if the Church made any change at all, that she would have put in something about the Anniversary of the Institution of the Holy Eucharist;

but no, the clause she inserts is about the Betrayal. She would have us remember that today is the Anniversary of the day on which He was betrayed. Presently we are reminded of it again by a deviation from her accustomed ritual;—the "Kiss of Peace," after the "Agnus Dei," is not given. There is no need for the Church to explain why; we know she would have us remember the base kiss given in the garden today, and we shudder at the thought of the treacherous priest.

Thus would the Church, in the midst of all our joy and thanksgiving for the Holy Eucharist, give us a note of warning. Judas was present at the first Mass; Judas received Holy Communion; and Judas betrayed his Master. The "Epistle" accentuates the thought, and gives us some practical advice. It is possible to eat the Bread (as the laity) or even to drink the chalice (as the Priest) unworthily, and to be guilty, as Judas was, of the Body and Blood of the Lord. How can we guard against this terrible sin? "Let a man prove himself, and so let him eat of that bread and drink of the chalice." Let us make sure, that is, that from head to feet we have been washed and pronounced "clean" by Him Who said so sorrowfully today: "You are clean, but not all."

Point II.

The "Hanc igitur"

"In memory of the day on which Our Lord Jesus Christ delivered to His disciples the mysteries of His Body and Blood to be celebrated." These are the words which the Church adds to the prayer beginning "Hanc igitur." We tell Him that we offer Him these Holy Mysteries in memory of what He did for us today. What did He do? He "left us a memorial of His Passion." He said so Himself: "This do ye for the commemoration of Me," and of what I suffered. Though our JESUS has died, He has left us a memorial. He has made His Will (the "New Testament"), and we have not been forgotten in it. today is the anniversary of the day on which He left that precious legacy for us. How tenderly we regard mementos of our loved ones! They remind us of them and of all that we have lost and call forth our gratitude at the thought that they did not forget us. But with the joy and gratitude sorrow mingles, and the very sight of the little token of love is sometimes more than we can bear. So it is, too, with the memento that our JESUS has left us, for it cannot but remind us of His sufferings, and of the part we had in causing them. But He turns all the sorrow into joy, for His memento is Himself! Lest we should forget, the Priest reminds us, every time that we receive It, that It is indeed the Body of the Lord. "Corpus Domini nostri JESU Christi"—"Corpus Domini nostri JESU Christi." He repeats it to each one. Could He have left us anything better than Himself to recall the memory of Himself?

With what love and gratitude should I receive, and always treat, His precious memento! It will be resting on the Altar of Repose today; let me spend all the time I can there, pouring out my soul in thanksgiving for this sweet Memorial of His Passion.

POINT III.

THE "QUI PRIDIE"

"Who the day before He suffered *for our salvation, and that of all mankind, that is, on this day,* took bread," etc. The words in *italics* are those added by the Church today to the *Prayer of Consecration.* Never on any other day does she make any change in the "*Qui pridie*." She would remind us that today is the very day—"the day before He suffered for our salvation"—that He took bread and broke it. He *Himself* broke the bread. He laid down His Own life, and gave to His disciples the same Body which suffered and died. "Take, eat, this is My Body." And then the Church goes on to "*show the death of the Lord*," for it is principally at the moment of Consecration that it is shown. The Priest consecrates *separately* the Body and the Blood, thus showing mystically the death that was caused by the actual separation of Body and Blood on the Cross. And though our Jesus "dieth no more"—for His Body and Blood, His Soul and His Divinity are for ever inseparable—yet He would have us *show* His death "for *a*, memorial." As all the Jewish sacrifices showed His death by pointing forwards, and saying: Remember, the Lamb of God is going to be sacrificed one day; so the Christian sacrifice shows His death by pointing backwards, and saying: "Christ our Pasch has been sacrificed for us, therefore let us keep the Feast." Let me think of this at the double Consecration; it should always remind me of the death of Jesus.

The Mass traces for us the Passion, line by line, if we will but look for it. Is it possible to see the Priest mixing water with the wine at the "Offertory" without thinking, not only of the Divine and the Human nature, but also of the Blood and Water which flowed from the precious wound in His Side? Is it possible to see the Body of the Lord lifted up at the "Elevation," without thinking of His own words: "I, if I be lifted up, will draw all men unto Me"? This is what our Jesus intended when He said that the Mass was to be "for a *Commemoration*"—a commemoration of all that He suffered for us.

How precious then is the Mass! By assisting at it we are in very deed standing with Mary at the Foot of the Cross.

Maundy Thursday is no interruption of Holy Week—rather does it emphasise it and extend it, showing us how we can, if we will, always be in Holy Week, always go to Calvary and see represented the great Action that took place there. We can always be sure of finding Mary there, and of receiving her smile of welcome as we come to take up our stand with her at the Foot of the Altar Cross.

Am I there as often as I might be? And if so, am I seeing to it that I am *no* disinterested spectator, but one for whom these things are a tremendous reality as well as an unspeakable consolation?

Colloquy. "We beseech Thee, O Holy Lord, Almighty Father, Eternal GOD, that JESUS Christ, Thy Son, Our Lord, Who on this day directed *(monstravit)* His disciples, by the surrender *(traditione)* of Himself, to do this in remembrance of Him, may make our sacrifice acceptable to Thee." (The "Secret.")

Resolution. To hear Mass well.

Spiritual Bouquet. "O Sacred Banquet, in which Christ is received, *the memory of His Passion* is renewed, the mind is filled with grace, and a pledge of future glory is given unto us."

— ❧ —

Events of the Day for Contemplation

Maundy Thursday.

1. It is the first day of Unleavened Bread; tonight the paschal lamb must be eaten in Jerusalem.
2. JESUS leaves Bethany for the last time to go up and keep the Feast according to the law.
3. He sends Peter and John to prepare the Passover, giving them a sign by which they may know the house.
4. Later on in the day He goes there with the twelve.
5. He eats the Passover in haste with His disciples—the lamb, the herbs, the unleavened bread.
6. The Social Banquet.
7. The Washing of the disciples' feet.
8. The Last Supper, at which He institutes the Holy Eucharist and the Christian Priesthood. John leans on His Breast, and the sop is dipped.
9. Judas goes out.
10. On leaving the Guest Chamber the Apostles dispute as to which of them shall be the greatest.
11. JESUS goes with His disciples to the Mount of Olives and gives the discourse on the Vine, and promises the Holy Ghost.
12. His prayer to His Father.
13. The Agony in the Garden.
14. The Betrayal with a kiss.
15. The Arrest and the chains.
16. The disciples forsake Him.
17. He is taken bound to Annas, where He receives the blow.

— ❧ —

After The Ninth Hour

Good Friday

"They shall look upon Me Whom they have pierced. They shall mourn for Him as one mourneth for an only son, and they shall grieve over Him, as the manner is to grieve for the death of the first-born. . . . And in that day there shall be a fountain opened." (Zach. xii. 10 and xiii. 1.)

1st *Prelude.*   The Mother of Sorrows.
2nd *Prelude.*   Grace to stand by, and watch, as Mary did.

POINT I.
THE FIFTH WOUND

Mary's quiet vigil by the dead Body of her Son is at length interrupted by the arrival of fresh soldiers coming on a cruel errand of mercy. They have been sent by Pilate to put an end to the misery of the criminals by breaking their legs. These are anxious moments for the Mother's heart, for as she watches the heavy blows dealt by the soldiers, she dreads any outrage to the Body of Jesus. The good thief dies a holy death, for he has the consolation of Mary's presence and prayers till his happy soul goes to be *with Jesus.* The bad thief will have none of these things, and to all appearances—though the Church does not allow her children to pass judgment on any single soul—he goes, like Judas, to his own place.

"But after they were come to Jesus, when they saw that He was already dead, they did not break His legs." It was not from any motives of mercy that they refrained, but because they were being held back by an unseen Hand—the Hand that wrote the Scriptures. It was expressly ordered in the Old Law that the paschal lamb was to have no bones broken— and the Scripture must be fulfilled.

From the *Campion Missal and Hymnal*

But Mary's heart was not going to be spared. "One of the soldiers with a spear opened His side, and immediately there came out Blood and Water." And the Mother's heart was pierced with another sword. What reason could there be for this terrible outrage? (1) As a proof of His death—not only to the soldiers, who might otherwise be accused of not having done their duty; but also to all those who, not wishing to believe in the Resurrection, might say that He did not really die. (2) That the Scripture might be fulfilled which saith: "They shall look on Him Whom they pierced." (3) That the grace which, through all time, was to flow from the Cross into the Sacraments of Baptism and the Holy Eucharist, might be foreshadowed. (4) That the Sacred Heart might empty itself for men, and ever after remain open to receive them. (5) To give one more satisfaction to His excess of love by ensuring that every drop of His Blood was shed. *One* drop was enough for the world's salvation, but not enough to satisfy that Heart of love. John bore witness, and never forgot the sight, for the Sacred Heart was already specially dear to him. Longinus, the soldier who opened the Sacred Heart, never forgot it either, for later he joined the glorious army of martyrs.

What effect has this precious Fifth Wound upon men in general? What effect has it upon me? "O Sacred Heart! Thou lovest; Thou art not loved; would that Thou wert loved!"

POINT II.

THE TAKING DOWN FROM THE CROSS

Two other men arrive now. They also are sent by Pilate, but they are *friends* of the Crucified, and have permission to take down the Body and bury it. Joseph of Arimathea; and Nicodemus, a Ruler of the Jews, who had come to JESUS in the night watches, for instruction on the Kingdom of GOD.

Nicodemus, like Joseph, has made up his mind to be a *secret* disciple no longer. He brings with him a hundred pounds' weight of myrrh and aloes, while Joseph brings the fine linen and the winding-sheet. There is no time to be lost, for the sun is already sinking, and with sunset the Sabbath begins. Reverently and lovingly they take down the Body of their Master from the Cross, every touch of the wounds forcing them to make reparation for their cowardice. They give the Crown of thorns and the nails to Mary; and presently they give her the Precious Body Itself, and another sword pierces her loving heart.

It is thirty-three years since she took Him in her arms for the first time, when His smile rewarded her for all. No less tenderly and wonderingly does she take Him now. There is no smile this time to greet her, and she weeps as she reads on the dead Body of her Child the story of His terrible sufferings, written in letters of blood. She needs no one to tell her, she sees for herself the marks of the blows, of the cords, of the scourges, of the thorns, of the Cross on His shoulder, of the nails and of the spear. She knows all now. And this is the best gift that GOD can find for the most perfect, the most faithful, the most tenderly loved of all His creatures! When shall I learn that suffering and sorrow are marks of GOD's special favour for His children?

Let me look again at the Mother, sitting there with the dead Body of her Son resting on her knees, and learn all I can from the picture. How much she is able to bear! It is her great love that gives her strength—love for GOD and His Holy Will. Those who love GOD most, can suffer most for Him.

Mary calls me near and bids me look. See, she says, how He has borne your griefs and carried your sorrows; you cannot be like Him unless you suffer. Look what sin has done to my Son! And as I look, I can bear it no longer, I fall on my

From the *Campion Missal and Hymnal*

knees and confess the truth: It was my sin. *I* did it. I am guilty of His Blood! When I look up again, Mary does not drive me away from her, as well she might. All she says is: I knew it, my child, and He knew it too, and all He wants now is that you should be sorry, and make reparation by your love. You have already given Him consolation by the humble confession of your sin.

Point III.

The Embalming and the Burial

Now Mary entrusts the Precious Body to the care of the disciples, and they carry it to the *Stone of Anointing*. Having washed the wounds, they wind tightly round the Sacred Body the fine linen saturated in the spices, and cover all with the winding-sheet. Does Mary think of the day when "she wrapped Him up in swaddling-clothes and laid Him in a manger"?

Why did Jesus permit all this to be done to His Body, which, on account of the Hypostatic union, could "never see corruption"? It was not only that He would, to the very end, be "made like unto His brethren," but also, because He wanted to give them a *proof* of His death. He knew that there would not be lacking those who said that His Resurrection was no miracle, because He was never dead. But no one could say that, about an embalmed body, for the process of embalming is also a process of suffocation.

The embalming of the Body of Jesus is not only a proof of His loving forethought, but also a reminder of a service that I can render to Him. I, too, have some embalming to do, for the Body of my Lord when It is under my care. Let me see to it that I have ready the sweet spices of humility, purity, charity, contrition, and any other whose perfume I know He specially loves, to wrap round His Sacred Body while It lies in my heart after Holy Communion.

The Stone of Anointing was close by the garden where Joseph's new tomb was hewn in the rock. There the little company of mourners gently lays to rest the Precious Body. They take a last farewell, falling on their faces to adore. They roll the great stone to the door of the sepulchre, and leave Him surrounded by adoring Angels.

All is finished; and as Mary turns to go home with her adopted son, the sun sets, the Great Sabbath has begun. "God ended His work, and He rested on the seventh day from all His work which He had done." (Gen. ii. 2.)

Let me come, my Mother, and share John's privilege, for I, too, am your child. I can see your heart pierced through and through with many swords, but I know that each one only unites it still more closely to the Heart of your Son. Let me stay with you and try to learn what the love of God's Will can do for those who surrender their own wills entirely to Him.

Colloquy with the Mother of Sorrows.

Resolution. To stand by, and watch with her today.

Spiritual Bouquet. "O all ye that pass by the way, behold and see."

Events of the Day for Contemplation

Good Friday

1. Jesus is sent (probably soon after midnight) to Caiaphas, who, after having found Him guilty of death, leaves Him in the Guard-room or Prison in charge of the servants and guards, till the morning.
2. Peter denies His Master.
3. As soon as it is day, Caiaphas assembles the whole Sanhedrin, who ratify the sentence illegally passed during the night, and then take Jesus to Pilate, to be put to death.
4. Judas returns his money, and goes and hangs himself.
5. Pilate sends Jesus to Herod, who mocks Him.
6. Herod sends Him back, dressed in a fool's garment, to Pilate.
7. Barabbas is preferred to Jesus.
8. The Scourging.
9. The Crowning with thorns.
10. The *Ecce Homo.*
11. The sentence of death.
12. The Way of the Cross.
13. The Crucifixion on Calvary. *Calvary* means *the place of a skull.* Tradition says that the skull was Adam's, that the Cross of Jesus stood over his tomb, and that the Precious Blood ran down on to his skull. This is why, from very early days, a skull has often been put at the foot of the Crucifix. (SS. Basil, Ambrose, Epiphanus, Jerome, Chrysostom, and Origen uphold this opinion.)
14. The death of Jesus.
15. The piercing of His Sacred Side.

16. He is taken down from the Cross and put in His Mother's arms.
17. His Body is embalmed and put into a new tomb, and a great stone is rolled to the entrance.
18. His Soul descends to Limbo.

The Great Sabbath Day

Holy Saturday.

"You have a guard; go, guard it as you know. And they departing, made the sepulchre sure, sealing the stone, and setting guards." (St Matt. xxvii. 65, 66.)

1ˢᵗ *Prelude.* The Sepulchre.
2ⁿᵈ *Prelude.* Grace to spend today with JESUS and Mary.

POINT I.
THE TOMB

"That was a great Sabbath Day." (St John xix. 31.) Never had there been a greater. The first Sabbath Day was great, when GOD rested after His work of Creation; but greater was that on which He rested after His work of Redemption. All was still, silent, hushed—for GOD, with that mortal Body which He took as an instrument of our salvation, was resting in the tomb.

The humiliation is all over now. JESUS has been buried as a rich man—as a King. The linen He was wrapped in was of the finest, the spices were costly, the tomb was not that of a poor man, for again there was a Scripture to be fulfilled: "He made His grave with the rich." Not long will His Body remain there; but long enough to leave its impression, with all the wounds, upon the winding-sheet, rendering it of priceless value.

Let me go to the Sepulchre today and "see this that has come to pass, which the Lord hath showed" to me. I see the soldiers whom the Chief Priests, with Pilate's permission, have placed on guard to prevent any attempt to steal the Body. I see the great stone rolled up against the entrance; and sealed, so that no one may tamper with it. But I cannot stay outside; my place is within, with the adoring Angels; yea,

I may approach even nearer than they, for the Body of my Lord, lying there on the cold, hard rock, speaks to me in a way it cannot speak to them. As I kneel in adoration it seems to draw me to It, till I feel that It is mine, and mine only. The Sepulchre is my heart, which once was intended by me for no one but myself; hard it was, as the rock; and cold, as the stone slab. But all is changed since He said: "My child, give *Me* thy heart." I went then, and "begged the Body of JESUS," and when, by my love and contrition and gratitude, I had taken It down from the Cross, I brought all the sweetest and costliest spices, hoping, by my sacrifice, to make my heart a little less unworthy to receive Him. But when the preparations were all finished, they seemed so inadequate, that I cried out: "Lord, I am not worthy that Thou shouldest come!" But nevertheless He came, saying: "My delights are to be with the children of men"; it was to make it possible for Me to come to you that I suffered and died. You make up to Me for all I suffered, when you take Me at My word and receive Me into your heart.

O my JESUS, make me like the winding-sheet when I receive Thee in Holy Communion. May I hold Thee so close that there is room for nothing between us, so close that the impress of Thyself is left upon me.

As I linger at the tomb today, let me ask myself: What is the result of my Communions? Is the impression of JESUS crucified so imprinted upon my heart, that there is an ever-increasing likeness in me to Him? Can others recognize the touch of the Body of JESUS, by my humility, my spirit of mortification and self-sacrifice, my gentleness and my charity? It is because I have touched the Body of His Son that GOD sets such an infinite value upon me. I am one of His *relics,* and on the day when He looks over His "special possessions," all those who have been, in any way, identified with JESUS, will find a place amongst them, and He "will spare them as a man spareth his son that serveth Him." (Mal. iii. 17.)

But there is yet another thought for me before I leave the Holy Sepulchre. In that Sacred Body, stretched on the rock, the *natural* life is no more; only the Divine Life is there. It is a picture of what my life ought to be—a tomb, where I, its inhabitant, lie dead, dead to sin, dead to my old nature; but a tomb where GOD lives and reigns, and where I am "alive unto GOD." Is such a supernatural life possible? Yes, but it can only be attained by the interior silence, peace, and recollection which the tomb of JESUS teaches me.

Point II.

LIMBO

While the Sacred Body joined to the Divinity is resting in the tomb; while the Precious Blood, wherever It is spilt, is being carefully guarded by adoring Angels—for It, too, is joined to the Divinity—the Holy Soul of JESUS, also joined to the Divinity, is full of life and activity. "*He descended into Hell,*" that is, into *Limbo*—the abode of the Just—to visit those souls for whom His own Human Soul was yearning, because they had been faithful to the promise of His coming, because they had been redeemed by His Blood and saved by Its merits, even before It was shed. There, since the arrival of Abel, some four thousand years ago, all those "who died according to faith, not having received the promises, but beholding them afar off, and saluting them," (Heb. xi. 13), had, since their Purgatory, been waiting. They had been waiting for the "Desired of all nations" to come, waiting for the great Sacrifice, to which, all through their lives, they had looked forward, and which was to open to them the gates of the Kingdom of Heaven. Constantly they had been cheered by the arrival of their brethren, each one bringing news of what was going on, on earth. Gradually the prophecies of the Messias had been growing less dim, and more detailed, since the days when Abraham, Isaac, Moses, Job, Elias, had entered Limbo. And during the last thirty years they had heard of prophecies being *fulfilled*. Simeon and Anna had been able to tell them that the "*Child was born, the Son given.*" (Isaias ix. 6.) The flock of baby martyrs had brought unspeakable joy into Limbo, for their flight straight from earth into "Abraham's bosom," without any sojourn in Purgatory, was a proof that the *Little Child* was already *leading*. (Isaias xii. 6.) Since then, these Prisoners of hope had heard many stories of the wonderful Child Who lived in Nazareth, and they would remember that He was to be called *Wonderful*. (Isaias ix. 6.) It was a great day for them when St. Joseph came among them! His silent tongue was unloosed when he got to Limbo; and he had so much to tell of Jesus and Mary, that Heaven's gates seemed already opening; his listeners almost forgot that they were in Limbo. Later on, John the Baptist told them of "the Lamb of God, Who taketh away the sins of the world"; of His Baptism, and of the Voice from Heaven; of His public ministry just begun. And then, when expectation was at its height, the beautiful Soul of the God-Man Himself appeared, filling all Limbo with such a flood of light that it was changed at once into Paradise. Happy souls! they were "with Jesus" at last, their banishment was over!

"Eye hath not seen, O God, besides Thee, what things Thou hast prepared for those that wait for Thee." (Isaias lxiv. 4.) Only He knows how He made up to these just ones for all their weary time of waiting, how He rendered to these Prisoners of hope *double* for all they had suffered. (Zach. ix. 12.) St Peter tells us that "He preached to those spirits in prison," (1 Pet. iii. 19), and we may well believe that "beginning at

Moses and all the prophets, He expounded to them in all the Scriptures the things that were concerning Him," (St Luke xxiv. 27), expounding to the Prophets themselves their own prophecies, and showing them, by the story of His Life and Death, how every "jot and tittle" had been fulfilled. While they were listening, another soul joined the blessed company—the first to be welcomed, by JESUS Himself —Dismas, the penitent thief, was *with JESUS in Paradise.*

"That was a great Sabbath day." Great, for the Holy Souls, for it never ended, and it never will. As I meditate about it, my thoughts cannot but turn again to my Communions, to my *great* days, to the moments when I, too, am *"with JESUS,"* and receive the pledge of my immortality.

POINT III.

CONSOLATRIX AFFLICTORUM

"Blessed are they that mourn, for they shall be comforted." Why has Saturday been specially dedicated to Mary? Surely because of her work on that "great Sabbath Day," when she proved herself to be the *"Consolatrix afflictorum."* She was the chief mourner, and yet she mourned less than any; for, in spirit, she was with her Son in Paradise, and she alone had faith to believe that on the third day His Body would rise again from the tomb.

By her never-failing faith, courage, and love, the Blessed Mother is able to cheer all that come to her. To whom *can* they go for consolation if not to His own Mother? There is John, who craves to hear from her own lips that she has really taken him for her son; Magdalen, who is heart-broken, and feels that she must keep close to the Mother, who shared every thought and feeling with Him Whom she has lost; Peter, who cannot rest till he has told the Mother all about his base denial of her Son; all the others, who long to confess their cowardice to someone; Joseph and Nicodemus, Longinus, the Centurion, Veronica, Simon the Cyrenian, and many others, who, anxious to declare themselves on the side of the Crucified, take the quickest and the surest way—they go to Mary. And so they keep coming—to unburden themselves; to get her pardon; to be assured from her own lips that they have her Son's; to gain strength and consolation. And in return they tell her little details of all that He did, and said, and suffered—details which she may not know, and if she *does,* she will not interrupt, for she loves to hear them all again. And they bring her treasures which they know she will be glad to have—the seamless robe, Veronica's veil, the cloth with which He was blindfolded, the reed that He held in His Hands, perhaps a thorn from the Crown, or a thong from the scourges—even the water in which His wounds were washed. Everything is precious; and every moment they spend with her deepens their love for Him. How could it be otherwise? "Behold your Mother!" It was He Himself Who said it.

O Mary, sweetest Mother, behold *all* your children today—that great family for which your Son laid down His life. Plead for them on this last day of Lent, bring back those who are still wandering, that they, too, may be found *with* JESUS tomorrow.

And let me come, too, my Mother, and spend this last day with you. It will be a comfort to me to tell you of all my shortcomings. I have not been all to your Son that I meant to be when He said to me: "Behold, we go up"! And even if I have not actually denied or betrayed Him, still I can see so many things that I might have done to give Him pleasure which I have not done. And, in spite of all, He has been so good to me. I should like to tell you of all that He has said, and done, and suffered for me; of the difficulties which seemed insur-mountable, that He has helped me through; of the heavy crosses that He has borne with me; of the peace He has given me in the midst of storms; of the new light He has thrown upon suffering. I know you love to hear all these things, my Mother, you never weary of them. And to tell them increases my love both for you and for Him. And cannot *I* bring you something today which will remind you of your Son? I know how you must have loved Veronica's veil, and how touched you must have been by the likeness. Oh, may I, too, be able to touch your heart because you can see in mine some likeness to your Son !

    Colloquy with Mary, with whom I am waiting till the glad Easter dawns, when I shall be once more *with Jesus.*

    Resolution. To let nothing distract me from JESUS and Mary today.

    Spiritual Bouquet. "Consolatrix afflictorum, ora pro nobis."

Thoughts for Contemplation

1. The Stone being sealed.
2. The guard watching.
3. The adoring Angels keeping guard over the Sacred Body in the Tomb, and over the Precious Blood wherever It was shed.
4. The Cenacle.
5. Hell.
6. Purgatory.
7. Limbo.
8. Paradise.
9. Heaven.

CPSIA information can be obtained
at www.ICGtesting.com
Printed in the USA
BVHW042102240219
541012BV00005B/5/P